Consuming Desire

Consuming Desire

*Sexual Science and the Emergence
of a Culture of Abundance,
1871–1914*

Lawrence Birken

Cornell University Press

Ithaca and London

First published 1988 by Cornell University Press.

International Standard Book Number 0-8014-2058-X
Library of Congress Catalog Card Number 88-47719
Printed in the United States of America
Librarians: Library of Congress cataloging information
appears on the last page of the book.

The paper in this book is acid-free and meets the guidelines for
permanence and durability of the Committee on Production Guidelines
for Book Longevity of the Council on Library Resources.

Contents

Preface

Our culture invests an impressive amount of capital in sexual science. We go to the "sexperts" the way earlier generations went to priests, ministers, and rabbis, hoping for answers to our questions about marriage, about lust, about whether to have children. We want quick and reassuring advice, with apparently objective scientific grounding, about impotence, heterosexuality, homosexuality, venereal disease, and now, in this age of AIDS, about even life and death. But when and why did a science of sex emerge, and what does its existence mean for our civilization? In this book, I have attempted to answer these questions by going back to some original sources in sexual, psychoanalytic, evolutionary, and economic theory that shaped the ideological climate in which we live. My argument is that sexology emerged during the transition from a protoindustrial culture of production to a mass industrial culture of consumption at the end of the nineteenth and the beginning of the twentieth century. In examining this transition I have identified two key tendencies associated with it: the breakdown of sexual difference and the relativization of sexual taste. The sexologists of that roughly fifty-year period, building on the epoch-making work of Charles Darwin, sought to fight these tendencies, even as they inadvertently furthered them. Consequently, I believe, sexual science has come to be associated with what is ultimately a project for extending the democratic model of society to its furthest conceivable limit by abolishing the distinctions between adults and children and between male and female.

Readers will recognize that what insights I have about sexology depend on my understanding of that "science" in a much larger sociohistorical context. This perspective derives from several sources. I am, of course, much indebted to the work of Traian Stoianovich, especially the idea (implicit in my whole argument) that Western culture has unique structural and ideological characteristics such as feudalism which first appeared in Northwest Europe as early as the eleventh century. Within this theoretical framework, I have situated a tripartite periodization of Western culture drawn from American writers such as David Riesman and French writers such as Jean Baudrillard, who seem to distinguish consecutive "feudal," "productivist," and "consumerist" phases of that culture. Within this more elaborate theoretical context I have adopted two types of analytic technique: first, the individualist/holist distinction employed by Louis Dumont as well as by Marxists and by modernization theorists such as W. W. Rostow, who believe in progressive "stages of growth," and, second, the "deconstruction" perspective used by Michel Foucault and his followers. Indeed, Foucault's analytical techniques have been central in shaping my commitment to the historization of ideology which I place at the center of any attempt to create a new intellectual history.

To Traian Stoianovich, whose enthusiasm and support for my work have long sustained me, I owe a personal as well as an intellectual debt. John Gillis was immensely useful in offering suggestions, reading numerous drafts, and encouraging me to go on with my work when this project was still in its early stages. Nina Shapiro was instrumental in calling to my attention the contradictions of late nineteenth-century economic thought. By sharpening my perception of the economic, she enabled me better to understand the character of

Western intellectual history in general. Harold Poor has long been an interested and informative critic (in the best sense of the word) of my views on the "sexual question." William Leach read several drafts of this work and especially encouraged me to link intellectual more thoroughly to social history. It was with this encouragement that I wrote Chapter 6. Peter Agree, my editor, has guided me through the long process of turning a manuscript into a book, patiently answering my questions and calming my fears. Finally, the late Warren Susman stimulated my interest in many of the issues raised in this work. First as a teacher and then as a friend, he provided both intellectual and spiritual inspiration. I will always cherish the memory of his kindness.

LAWRENCE BIRKEN

New Brunswick, New Jersey

Consuming Desire

Introduction

These chapters are shaped by the conviction that sex is profoundly important in contemporary culture. Moreover, I believe that this importance, applauded by some and decried by others, has never been adequately explained. In part, this is because we have been too overwhelmed by the fact of sex. But sex as an activity has always existed. What is new about our culture is its invention of a "science" of sex, a sexual ideology that is somehow symbolic of the way in which our social order is constructed. For many scholars, the emergence of "sexology" signals a step forward in the progressive development of Western civilization. This liberal, and probably mainstream, view was expressed by Paul Robinson in his *Modernization of Sex*; Robinson assumes that the expansion of sexual discourse is symptomatic of a genuine liberation. It was precisely this view that Michel Foucault challenged in his *History of Sexuality: An Introduction*. If Robinson associated the emergence of a science of sex with sexual freedom, Foucault saw that science as a new form of sexual tyranny. In arguing against the "liberal" conviction that sex was repressed during the eighteenth and nineteenth centuries only to be liberated by sexology in the twentieth, Foucault was actually arguing that the modern idea of sex itself was historically constituted as a form of repression by sexology. A useful corrective to Robinson's liberalism, Foucault's assessment of sexual science is nevertheless too negative. To a great extent, this negative assessment is a function of his understanding of ideology in general. For Foucault, any ideology, any theory, any form of cultural discourse whatever implies a limitation of possibilities. In fact, from a Foucauldian perspective, all conceivable forms of sociocultural organization must be repressive simply because they are organizations. From such a perspective, the emergence of sexual discourse is simply the emergence of one more form of control in an increasingly complex civilization. The more discussion of sex, the less freedom. Reduced to its essentials, of course, Foucault's position is untenable because it implies that all theories (including his own) function as grids of control. The extreme relativism of his position thus relativizes itself out of existence.[1]

Nevertheless, from this position we can extract certain insights. In particular, Foucault forces us to ask ourselves not only why the West alone produced a sexual science but, more generally, why the West produced science at all. Foucault himself did not live long enough to answer these questions in any satisfactory way. In this book, therefore, my aim is to go beyond Foucault's work and find my own answers. In the following chapters, I hope to show that sexology is an ideology par excellence by placing it in the larger context of Western thought. Moreover, I want to suggest that the history of sexual science represents the culmination of a very long process of development in the West.[2]

1. Michel Foucault, *The History of Sexuality: An Introduction* (New York: Vintage, 1980); see also Paul Robinson, *The Modernization of Sex: Havelock Ellis, Alfred Kinsey, William Masters and Virginia Johnson* (New York: Harper & Row, 1976).

2. For an excellent discussion of Foucault's view on the tyrannical character of ideology, see Rebecca Comay, "Excavating the Repressive Hypothesis," *Telos* 67 (Spring 1987), 111–20.

I

A popular dictionary defines ideology as "the body of ideas reflecting the social needs and aspirations of an individual, group, class or culture."[3] Although this definition is serviceable enough, I would prefer one more grounded in our shared cultural experience. I hypothesize that the origins of the ideology of "science" in the West can be tied, in part, to the tendency here for knowledge to outgrow faith. In his excellent study of social laws, Robert Brown noted the connection between the idea of a Divine Legislator and the emergence of a conception of a lawful universe.[4] If Brown is correct, one condition for the emergence of modern science may have been the belief in a creator who lawfully orders the world. But this idea the West shared with Byzantium and Islam. What was unique about the West and, I suspect, important in its development of a natural law was the revolt against that creator. It happened something like this: the success of feudalism, whose faith was received from the church, led to an increase in wealth, trade, and contact with the East. Increased contact with the East led to a revival of classical knowledge, much of which was not so much absorbed into the Christian synthesis as made the basis for a parallel protoscientific culture. According to Francis Schaeffer, alongside the concept of a divine revelation bestowed by the Bible (via the first or priestly order of feudal society), a conception of a second or "natural" revelation eventually appeared. At the beginning of the Renaissance, nature was first studied as a way of understanding God. Here was the probable genesis of the central idea that, because God was lawful, his creation was lawful too. By the end of the Renaissance, however, the study of nature had become increasingly an end in itself and

3. *The American Heritage Dictionary of the English Language* (Boston: Houghton Mifflin, 1981).

4. Robert Brown, *The Nature of Social Laws: From Machiavelli to Mill* (Cambridge: Cambridge University Press, 1984), pp. 1–23.

thus a subtle form of revolt against God. There is thus something to be said for the thesis that the gradual banishment of God from nature led to a kind of cultural vacuum in the West, a vacuum filled by the increasing emphasis on the lawful, self-regulating character of the natural (under which must be subsumed the social) world.[5]

In the course of its development, then, Western thought gradually replaced a transcendent divine with an immanent natural law. I would further suggest, if only provisionally, that this gradual extension of natural law took place within the context of a continuous redefinition and expansion of a "democratic" model of society, a model whose ultimate origins may be found in the aristocratic idea of the peer (equal). To be more technical, the movement from a transcendent divine to an immanent natural law occurred within the framework of a profound shift from a holistic (or caste) to an individualistic (or class) conception of the social order. According to social theorist Louis Dumont, holist ideologies assume that the various parts of society were different from one another from the start, so that people born into those parts of society were also different from the start. In contrast, individualistic ideologies assume that people were similar from the start and only become different through a process of differentiation and specialization. In a holistic society, then, the barriers between the castes or orders appear to be relatively impermeable, and the distinctions between them qualitative. Moreover, the several parts of society are sustained by a mythology of an eternal *difference* between them. In more individualistic societies, the several parts of society are separated by barriers that are relatively permeable, and the distinctions between these parts are basically quantitative. Ideologically, such societies need be supported only by myths of a historical *differentiation* of

5. These ideas are developed in an interesting way in Francis A. Schaeffer, *Escape from Reason* (Downer's Grove, Ill.: Intervarsity Press, 1968), pp. 7–29.

classes from an original unity. Indeed, the assumption of an underlying similarity between individuals has been an essential axiom of the discourses of liberty and equality which have become increasingly central to Western thought since the Middle Ages.[6]

Western history, then, is the history of "democratization," of a dissolution of holism in favor of individualism. In the feudal epoch, a natural inequality between aristocracy and commonality was assumed. The feudal ideology of the three functions of society—war, prayer, and work—(somewhat analogous, if Georges Dumézil is correct, to the ideology of the four varnas that prevailed on the Indian subcontinent) founded this inequality on the eternal *difference* between the several functions of society and the people within them. But within the aristocracy itself, the elements of a counter-ideology of liberty and equality among peers existed. Such an ideology of a citizenship based on power is perhaps found in the earliest social science, that of Machiavelli. Political science certainly emerged as the first domain of individual action, the first domain in which holistic conceptions were banished in favor of an individualism of power. Yet, this individualism was still restricted to the aristocratic castes of prayer and war.[7]

In the mid-seventeenth century, however, John Locke began the construction of a new domain of knowledge associated with the emergence of a "bourgeois" perspective. Just as Machiavelli saw political sovereignty and autonomy as the criterion for an aristocratic individualism of power, Locke discovered property as the basis for what C. B. Mac-

6. See Louis Dumont, *Homo Hierarchicus: The Caste System and Its Implications*, trans. Mark Sainbury (Chicago: University of Chicago Press, 1974), especially p. 9.

7. For a discussion of the emancipation of the political realm and the significance of Machiavelli, see Louis Dumont, *Essays on Individualism: Modern Ideology in Anthropological Perspective* (Chicago: University of Chicago Press, 1986), especially pp. 71–72, 83; see also Niccolo Machiavelli, *The Prince*, trans. Robert Adams (New York: Norton, 1977), especially Adams's introduction, pp. xvii–xviii.

pherson has called "possessive individualism" based on labor. Just as Machiavelli posited a political world composed of heroic individuals, Locke began the construction of a new and wider domain peopled by calculating individuals. In the decades immediately preceding the French Revolution, eighteenth-century thinkers such as Adam Smith and François Quesnay built upon the new conception of individualism, carving out a heretofore unknown "economic" domain.[8]

Beginning with Locke, the myth of the eternal difference between the three orders of society was apparently abolished. In the *Second Treatise*, the liberty and equality of possessive individuals are traced to their original and, thus, natural similarity at the beginning of time. On the surface, Locke and his successors articulated a bourgeois ideology that banished the warrior and the priestly castes, and thus caste itself, from society, apparently totally replacing holism with individualism. But as numerous scholars have recognized, this bourgeois individualism rigorously excluded the family from its domain. In the political economy, there could be only one will representing each household, and that will was the father's. For between men and women, an eternal *difference* appeared to block the inclusion of the latter in the political economic world of the former. A male/female caste system founded on the perceived natural difference between the sexes thus replaced the older three-function caste system of the aristocratic epoch. So pervasive was the bourgeois assumption of an eternal natural difference between the sexes that even critics of the bourgeois sexual order such as Marx and Mill still half-accepted it.[9]

8. C. B. Macpherson, *The Political Theory of Possessive Individualism: From Hobbes to Locke* (Oxford: Oxford University Press, 1983).

9. John Locke, *The Second Treatise of Government* (London: Basil Blackwell, 1966), p. 41; also see Traian Stoianovich, "Gender and Family: Myths, Models, and Ideologies," *History Teacher* 15 (November 1981): 67–117. See Donald Lowe, *The History of Bourgeois Perception* (Chicago: University of Chicago Press, 1984), pp. 70–74, for a discussion of the public masculine versus the private feminine space during this period. See Mary O'Brian,

Actually, it was Darwin who, however unwittingly, really challenged that order. Whereas the radical conceptions of society advanced by both Mill and Marx were limited by the existence of two sexes as a fact of biology, Darwin redefined biology itself. If Machiavelli discovered power as the underlying basis of the political realm, and if Locke discovered labor as the unifying substance of the political-economic realm of the male sex, Darwin discovered desire as the fundamental ground of both sexes. By making this discovery, he became the real founder of sexology, the forerunner of the sexologists in the same way that Locke was the precursor of the economists. With Darwin, a new domain of knowledge appeared, one inhabited by desiring individuals. In this context, Freud, despite his genius, appears to be merely the most talented of Darwin's numerous intellectual progeny. For example, it appears that Freud extended the definition of sex in two significant and interrelated ways; first, he assigned a definite sexuality to women and children; second, he included many abnormal or "perverted" forms of behavior in his definition. But it turns out that "sexualization" was really implicit in Darwinism from the beginning. With its hypothesis of a common origin for all life, evolutionary monism subverted the distinctions both between male and female and between heterogenitality and perversion. In the Darwinian state of nature, there were only genderless, desiring creatures. Darwinism thus struck a blow against the idea of an eternal, qualitative difference between the two sexes, banishing holism from the family, its last refuge. Here, indeed, was the elemental basis for a new conception of individualism based on desire itself, an individualism including men and women, adults and chil-

---

"Reproducing Marxist Man," in Lorenne Clark and Lynda Lange, eds., *The Sexism of Social and Political Theory* (Toronto: University of Toronto Press, 1979), pp. 99–116, for an analysis of Marxism as an ideology of the masculine sphere. See also Richard R. Krouse, "Mill and Marx on Marriage, Divorce, and the Family," *Social Concept* 1 (September 1983).

dren, since all could now be regarded as fundamentally the same. The sexualization of women and children, implicit in Darwin, thus signaled the extension of the democratic or individualist model to the furthest limit.[10]

II

If Western natural law has implied a kind of regulation without overt coercion, an immanent rather than a transcendent law, then the progressive extension of this "deregulation" has created a paradoxical situation. At each step, natural law has attempted to take away the freedoms it has given, closing the Pandora's box it has opened. Thus, even Machiavelli emancipated politics from theology only to reduce the political to a set of rules. This paradox becomes ever more evident in more recently constituted systems of natural law. Locke and his successors carved out a new political domain by emancipating property from theology. In the process, they made property the new criterion for citizenship, at least within the masculine sphere of political economy. But having banished inequality, at least from the masculine sphere, Locke and his successors partially restored it by delineating the way in which inequality in property historically arose. Political thinkers in the eighteenth and nineteenth centuries used this theory of possessive individualism to justify the exclusion from power of relatively poorer males who were understood to be the technical, though not actual, equals of their richer brothers. But this new distinction among property-owners, between the class

10. For a more thorough discussion of this subject, see my article "Darwin and Gender," *Social Concept* 4 (December 1987); for more on erotic monism, see Alfred Kelly, *The Descent of Darwin: The Popularization of Darwinism in Germany, 1860–1914* (Chapel Hill: University of North Carolina Press, 1981). For the best overall survey tying Freud and the other sexologists to Darwinism, see Frank Sulloway, *Freud: Biologist of the Mind— Beyond the Psychoanalytic Legend* (New York: Basic, 1983).

of men who owned real estate and the class of men whose only estate was their labor, was founded not on an eternal *difference* but on a historical *differentiation* from an original common sameness. Consequently, the new distinction functioned only as a partial reterritorialization, a sort of semipermeable social membrane.[11]

C. B. Macpherson has sketched out the contradictory treatment of poorer class in the work of Locke. The permeable nature of the barrier between the classes Locke and his successors constructed is obvious in several ways. Theoretically, the excluded or working classes occupied an ambivalent position. Included in the realm of citizens on the basis of their property in labor, excluded because their labor did not constitute *enough* property, they were disenfranchised ultimately on the basis of quantitative rather than qualitative considerations. The excluded classes were often denied the vote in the bourgeois epoch simply because they did not possess enough wealth, and wealth was just a matter of degree. By virtue of their ambivalent position, the poor were sometimes characterized by liberal and even revolutionary thinkers in the eighteenth century as "passive citizens," a term that embodies an internal contradiction. The same ambivalence was evident in political economy, which envisioned workers as self-interested economic individuals even as it stigmatized them as drudges. Practically, however, it was possible for people to move across class lines without legal sanction. It required no patent of nobility to transform a proletarian into a bourgeois or, for that matter, a bourgeois into a proletarian.[12]

From Locke on, then, caste was replaced by class with-

---

11. Locke, *Second Treatise*, pp. 14–27, provides the definitive account of the original equality within the masculine sphere of action; in the same way, Darwin provides the definitive account of the original identity or equality of the two sexes in his *Descent of Man, and Selection in Relation to Sex* (Princeton: Princeton University Press, 1981).

12. For the Lockean account of the contradictions within the masculine sphere, see Macpherson, *Possessive Individualism*, pp. 247 ff.

in the masculine sphere of political economy. In striking contrast, we have seen, caste survived in the form of the distinction between the sexes that was so salient a feature of bourgeois ideology. In all the states of nature theorized by Enlightenment thinkers, men and women are always *different from the very beginning*. But the emergence of Darwinism and its conception of what was nothing less than a genderless state of nature inhabited by transsexual organisms marked the beginning of the erosion of sex-caste and thus the appearance of a concept of a universal citizenship based on desire. From Darwin on, the barriers between the sexes erode, becoming semi-permeable rather than impermeable, quantitative rather than qualitative. Darwin and his followers, quite inadvertently, I suppose, created the basis for a universal concept of liberty and equality that could include individuals of both sexes, although they did so only by abolishing those sexes. Yet Darwin partially restored sexual inequality by explaining how two unequal sexes emerged out of a common hermaphroditic ancestry. In a kind of partial compensation, sexual *difference* was abolished, only to be replaced by a doctrine of sexual *differentiation* from a common sameness. To be sure, the new distinction between men and women postulated by Darwin afforded only an incomplete barrier against transsexuality and the universal citizenship based upon it. In the following chapters, I hope to demonstrate that the sexologists increasingly accentuated the post-Darwinian idea that "male" and "female" (and "normal" and "perverted") are fundamentally relative terms, and that each sex possesses remnants of the opposite sex so that sexuality is really a kind of spectrum of sexual types quantitatively rather than qualitatively distinct from one another.[13]

13. For the exclusion of women and children in Locke, see Lorenne Clarke, "Women and Locke: Who Owns the Apples in the Garden of Eden?", in Clarke and Lange, *Sexism*, pp. 16–40; for a broader view, see Linda Nicholson, *Gender and History* (New York: Columbia University Press, 1986), pp. 133–200. I agree with Stoianovich and Nicholson that the

The incomplete nature of this new system of sex distinctions envisioned by Darwin and his followers explains the ambivalent position occupied by women, as well as children and "perverts," within that system. Just as workers were simultaneously excluded from and included in the masculine sphere of political economic action that Locke and his successors delineated, so women, children, and perverts, however these categories might appear to differ from one another, were simultaneously excluded from and included in the universal sphere of sexuality that Darwin and his epigones constructed. In psychoanalysis, for example, women are simultaneously endowed with a libido, like the male, and regarded as receptive, unlike the male, thus appearing as the "passive citizens" of the erotic universe.[14]

III

I trust my readers will forgive my long excursion into our history. But it was necessary to define that history in a new way in order to explain how the "sex question" has come to occupy such an apocalyptic place in our culture. By

---

extreme separation of the two spheres was particularly characteristic of the bourgeois phase of Western culture and should not be regarded as a transhistorical fact. For example, the great functional distinction in Western aristocratic culture was that between the three orders. Only in the period after 1750 and before 1900 was this functional distinction reconceptualized as one between male and female. In turn, it is *this* system of distinctions that began to erode after Darwin.

14. The shift from a pre-Darwinian concept of difference to a post-Darwinian concept of differentiation between the sexes has been the subject of some discussion, although it is usually not recognized as such. In particular, Ivan Illich has seen a radical discontinuity between these two ways of organizing the sexes. In contrast, I have asserted that the idea of differentiation may be regarded as an eroded form or cultural "memory trace" of the older idea of difference. Put another way, the idea of differentiation is a partial reterritorialization of the older idea of difference, a kind of cultural compromise between the older idea and the newer possibility of abolishing difference altogether. See Ivan Illich, *Gender* (New York: Pantheon, 1982) and my review of that book in *Telos* 63 (Spring 1985).

recognizing the geneology of that culture, we see how the sexualization of women, children, and perverts appears as the latest step in a long process of democratization which began at the very dawn of Western culture and has been extended by degrees. Sexualization appears apocalyptic because it is symbolic of the extension of the democratic model of society to its furthest limit, a limit that from our perspective appears to be the end of Western civilization.

More specifically, this sexualization takes two specific forms: on the one hand, the recognition of the desires of women and children is symbolic of their emerging individualism; on the other hand, the recognition of the perversions as simple variations is symbolic of the new emphasis on radically idiosyncratic desire which is the basis for that individualism. Something deeply rooted in our culture confers on individuals this right of self-expression. To be sure, in earlier epochs, it was a right restricted to the relatively few. But in succeeding ages, its scope has been extended. Finally, in the course of the twentieth century, desire has begun to replace property as the symbolic badge of individualism. It is in this context that we must perceive a moral basis for the universally experienced but radically idiosyncratic desire that fuels the sexual revolution. The most varied sexual repertoire, the most abandoned promiscuity takes on a positive moral significance, however loath we are to admit it, in a culture in which the desire of the masses is as important as their labor.

Sexualization, then, is the newest phase of individualism. But we have seen that systems of natural law have come to exist in a kind of opposition to the very fields of individualism they open up; they are, in other words, partial reterritorializations, imposing an immanent law in those areas in which transcendence has been banished. In the West, natural law has implied a type of self-regulation apparently compatible with individual freedom. In this context, sexology takes on a particularly titanic significance because it appears as the last line of defense against a universal democratization and dissolution of the social order. Sexology, itself symbolic of the dissolution of holism, presents itself as the final barrier against the disintegration of the last remnant of holism embodied in the family. No wonder the whole "sexual question" is discussed in an increasingly charged atmosphere.

Against this background, the work begun by Darwin and elaborated by Krafft-Ebing, Havelock Ellis, and Freud more or less centered on the formulation of a natural law of sex. If classical political economy argued that the self-determination of the possessive individual was compatible with a self-renewing (masculine) productive order, the sexual science that emerged after Darwin implied that the self-determination of the genderless consuming individual was compatible with a self-renewing reproductive order that embraces both sexes. In general, by postulating that desire, in the healthy individual, inevitably leads to reproduction, sexology argued that the reproductive order was a self-regulating system. In other words, as transcendence was ejected from the sexual sphere, sexology elaborated an increasingly complex immanent law of sex to replace that vanishing transcendence.

It is not surprising that the sexologists sensed the strategic importance of their enterprise. If the slogan of the political economists had been "let the economy alone," the slogan of the sexual scientists might just as well have been "let the sexonomy alone." From the end of the nineteenth century, sexologists sought to subject a wide area of jurisprudence to the natural law of desire, thus emancipating the immanent law of sex from a legal system ultimately grounded in the assumption of transcendence. Havelock Ellis thus wrote of Krafft-Ebing that he was endowed "with the firm conviction that he was conquering a great neglected field of morbid psychology, which rightly belonged to the physician."[15] As

---

15. Havelock Ellis and John Addington Symonds, *Sexual Inversion* (London: Macmillan, 1987; rpt. New York: Arno Press, 1975), p. 29.

sexology developed, it contrived to decontrol large areas of sexual life. Yet, in so far as it withdrew from the overt regulation of sexuality, the state transferred its power to the plethora of psychiatrists, psychologists, sex therapists, and social workers who, armed with the new doctrines of sexual science, became the engineers of the autonomous "realm of sex." Thus Foucault was right in arguing that sexual science was a new discourse of control. But sexology also furthered the very individualism that it attempted to limit. And it is precisely Foucault's failure to recognize the two-sided and contradictory nature of sexual science that demands that we go beyond his analysis.

IV

In the following chapters, then, I intend to explore the structure of this sexology. I want to demonstrate in great detail that within sexology dwell two very different perspectives, one associated with productivist, the other linked with a more democratic consumerist point of view. Each perspective is characterized by its own complex of values. The first, harking back to the Englightenment and Locke, is gendered, work-oriented, and optimistic, whereas the second is genderless, play-oriented, and pessimistic. I am hypothesizing that sexology emerges during the transition from a production-oriented to a consumer-oriented culture. I further hypothesize that the contradictory structure of sexual science is actually an expression of its transitional nature. In other words, sexology simultaneously expresses consumerist values such as genderlessness and struggles against these very values. To illuminate this ambiguity, closely linked to the inability of twentieth-century culture to emancipate itself fully from nineteenth-century values, I have concentrated on the formative period of sexual science from 1871, when Darwin elaborated his theory of the genderless ancestry of mankind, to 1914, when Freud ratified the universalization of sex in the paper "On Narcissism," although relevant material from beyond these chronological limits may sometimes appear.

Because my fundamental interest here is, first, to delineate the contradictory structure of sexology in all its aspects, and, second, to situate that science in the larger history of Western thought, this book is basically a work in what is unfortunately called "intellectual history." My data are the ideas of the sexologists found in their books and articles, published between 1871 and 1914. I have also made use of similar materials from allied disciplines such as economics and evolutionary biology, in order to compare the ideological structure of those disciplines with that of sexual science. Not all my readers will be thoroughly sympathetic to my separation of ideas from the people who produced them. Yet we regularly study architecture without reference to the architect. I believe that ideas, as much as buildings, are cultural artifacts that can tell us about the societies that produce them. In the following chapters, I have attempted to understand sexology as ideology, even mythology. Instead of treating psychoanalysis and its intellectual cognates as tools, I have treated them as cultural artifacts. My characterization of sexology as ideology says nothing, however, in judgment on its scientific context. A body of ideas functions as an ideology when it acts as a symbolic representation of social relationships, *whatever* its scientific content. Science and ideology are not mutually exclusive.

I should stress that this essay does *not* constitute a sociological study of turn-of-the-century sexual life or a sociological, prosopographical, or biographical study of the early sexologists. These topics, however useful, provide short-run explanations. But I have decided to excise biography and sociology rather mercilessly from my history in order to understand better the long-run structure of that history. Indeed, my understanding of the shift in thought around 1900 as an aspect of a much longer process has dictated my methodology, a type of anthropology of Western intellectual history. Now, the type of history I propose implies that we can make sense out of historical change. We are confronted with the problem of accounting for the emergence of an ideology at a particular point in the development of Western culture. Why did sexology emerge when it did? Solving this problem presents many theoretical difficulties. One of the difficulties in dealing with the "rarified" cultural phenomena sometimes encountered when doing intellectual history is that they tend to be so widely and yet sparsely diffused that they are very hard to tie to any particular national or regional culture except in a very abstract and general way. Since sexology, from the beginning, has been a trans-national, or at least a transatlantic phenomenon, it is particularly hard for the historian to root it in any particular national or regional culture. Such a general phenomenon probably requires a relatively general explanation. I have attempted to find the common elements of Western cultures which might account for the simultaneous emergence of a sexological perspective in Europe and North America around 1900. But, of course, I can do this only by stating some general propositions about the development of Western culture.

Although it may be relatively easy to delineate the contradictions of sexual science and even to situate that science in the intellectual history of the West, any explanation of why that history developed the way it did must remain somewhat speculative. Early on, I concluded that neither the Marxism of the Frankfurt School nor the modernization theory of W. W. Rostow could provide such an explanation. Indeed, it is increasingly and, I think, correctly argued that both theories are residues of the bourgeois or productivist phase of Western culture. Precisely for this reason, neither Marxist nor modernization theory can grasp the essential character of the emerging consumer culture. The inadequacy of Marxism in this area was, in part, already understood by such thinkers as Stuart Chase, who in the 1930s continued to embrace a form of dialectical materialism even as he rejected Marxism as a philosophy of scarcity outmoded by the conditions of "abundance" obtaining by the end of the nineteenth century. More recently, Jean Baudrillard has criticized Marx for internalizing the very bourgeois or productivist values he set out to oppose in the first place. Productivist ideology, and the entire conception of a self-renewing sphere of production (economy), are a residue from a time when the propertied individual was assumed to be an active member of society and when individuality and citizenship were assigned to the essentially masculine domain of property. As Mary O'Brian has suggested, Marxist thought could not help but incorporate the structural separation of the sexes characteristic of the epoch in which Marx constructed his ideas. Just as Hegel excluded the family from history, Marx excluded reproduction from his materialism. But with the emergence of a truly genderless perspective after 1871, Marxist thought began to make some effort to assimilate the new concept of human nature implied by that perspective. Engels made a significant contribution in this direction with his attempt to expand the basis of history from production to include reproduction. But he ended up merely resolving the differentiation of the sexes into a form of the differentiation of the (masculine) sphere of the economy, thereby reasserting the primacy of the productivist perspective. Truly to transcend that perspective, Marxism would have had to declare itself a branch of Darwinism.[16]

16. See Stuart Chase, *The Economy of Abundance* (Port Washington, N.Y.: Kennikat, 1971); Jean Baudrillard, *The Mirror of Production* (St. Louis: Telos, 1975); Isaac Balbus, *Marxism and Domination: A Neo-Hegelian Feminist, Psychoanalytic Theory of Sexual, Political and Technological Liberation* (Princeton: Princeton University Press, 1982), pp. 11–60. For Marxism and gender, see O'Brian, "Reproducing Marxist Man," and Frederick Engels, *The Origin of the Family, Private Property and the State* (London: Lawrence & Wishart, 1973), pp. 71–72. For a further critique of the limitation of Marx's and Engels's approach to gender, see Shulamith Firestone, *The Dialectic of Sex* (New York: Bantam, 1970), a study that suggests the role of technology in eroding gender distinctions.

Marxists, like modernization theorists, thus tend to miss the radicality of consumer culture by reproducing the bourgeois tendency to dichotimize the world into a pre-capitalist and a capitalist epoch. Such a crude dichotimization of history also stands in the way of recognizing that the dissolution of holism in Western culture has proceeded in phases. Both Marxists and modernization theorists have, in particular, remained blind to the way holism was retained in the domain of gender even after being expelled from Western society elsewhere. Ultimately, these faults may be traced to the way both types of theorists remain obsessed with the primacy of the economic, an obsession that is itself a remnant of nineteenth-century culture.

One symptom of this obsession is the common tendency of both Marxists and modernization theorists to postulate a comparatively simplistic conception of causation linking economics to ideology. In these chapters, I do not reject the idea of historical determinism; such an idea is essential in any attempt to perceive an overall pattern of historical events. What I intend to transcend is the concept of a determinism that ties mode of production completely to social form. I intend to exclude this determinism by stressing the way the early history of the West helped determine its later development. Specifically, I shall argue that neither the productivist nor the consumerist form of Western culture can explain the development of individualism in that culture without taking into consideration the feudal context out of which these forms developed. My explanatory system thus operates both spatially (connecting mode of production and social formation) and temporally (stressing how the feudal genesis of Western culture helped shape that culture).

V

These considerations have helped shape the organization of this book, making a traditional, narrative, linear history out of the question. Rather, because the work is a study of a particular period of time which saw the emergence of a new ideology of desire, I try to demonstrate the existence of this new ideology in several different disciplines that formed simultaneously. If I give sexology a privileged position, it is only within the context of these other disciplines. Actually, the book is organized so that each of the following chapters represents a different perspective on the same emerging culture. I am thus interested in looking at a slice of history from several different directions. Because I proceed thematically rather than chronologically, narrative linearity disappears in favor of a kind of cubist simultaneity. And yet, even if my immediate concerns are structural, the ultimate context of this work is clearly historical. The first four chapters delineate the contradictory structure and the transitional character of late-nineteenth-century intellectual history. By way of introduction, Chapter 1 outlines the contradictions and structures of the new "marginalist" economics that emerged after 1871. Chapter 2 examines the way in which the contradictory structure of sexual science was analogous to that of marginalist economics. Chapters 3 and 4 explore the ambiguities of the evolutionary theories of sex, femininity, childhood, generation, and degeneration. In contrast to the first four chapters, the fifth is more explicitly historical. In effect, Chapter 5 attempts to trace the phases in the history of sexology, all the time understanding those phases as parts of a larger process, embracing numerous disciplines, in which the democratic model was redefined, nuanced, and extended. In a sense, Chapters 1–5 constitute a purely intellectual history in which I try to describe the structuring and destructuring of a particular phase in the history of Western thought. Chapter 6, in contrast, attempts to situate that thought in its broader sociohistorical context. This context, it turns out, is the movement from a protoindustrial culture of improvement to an industrial culture of mass consumption. Because the linking of ideas to their social context is even more difficult than the linking of

ideas to other ideas, I regard Chapter 6 as the most speculative part of the book. Finally, after a concluding seventh
chapter, I have added an epilogue focusing on the way the
contemporary critique of the sexual revolution challenges us
to assess the long-term significance of the emergence of
consumer culture in the United States.

VI

A final word: Perhaps the greatest obstacle to an understanding of the intellectual history of the late nineteenth and
early twentieth centuries is terminology. First, the transitional character of this history is reflected in the ambiguous
meaning of certain terms. Most readers will be familiar, for
example, with the old debate over whether Freud made
everything "sexual" or simply changed the meaning of
"sexual." Second, the problem of definition is complicated
by the historical distance between fin-de-siècle and contemporary culture. If we were dealing with either an earlier or a
more contemporary civilization, the terminology would
probably be easier to understand. In the former case, it
would clearly be unfamiliar; in the latter case, clearly familiar. But the study of ideas constructed in the late nineteenth
and early twentieth centuries requires us to master words
that sometimes appear familiar when they are unfamiliar,
and unfamiliar when they are familiar. Thus the term "sexuality" originally referred to one's own physiological sex,
only gradually taking on a secondary meaning relating to
sexual desire, a meaning embodied in the terms "heterosexuality" and "homosexuality." In the meantime, though,
theories had evolved linking sexual desire to physiology.
Such is our dilemma: terminology functions as a kind of
standard of measurement in intellectual history. When the
standard is itself changing, measurement becomes extremely
problematic. And, it should be remembered, in this case the
standard of measurement is itself part of the phenomenon

being measured. Part of the problem, of course, is simply that twentieth-century ideas have not yet been emancipated from nineteenth-century words. For example, Marxists and modernization theorists alike have tended to equate "market" with market economy, and "individualism" with possessive individualism. In effect, they have resolved all forms of individualism into bourgeois individualism. It is interesting that in his later work Foucault tended to absorb these attitudes too. In this context the emerging culture of desire is explained away even before it is given a hearing: it cannot be put into any but productivist language. Hence, the plethora of productivist metaphors for consumerist culture, metaphors such as "marketable personality," "sex-economy," and "political economy of sex," metaphors that reflect the idea that the economic is still central, metaphors whose metaphorical character is soon forgotten. It is for this reason that I have employed the term "sexonomy," originally suggested by Traian Stoianovich, to describe the domain of genderless consuming individuals investigated by sexual science. By using this term, I am implying that sexology signals a new phase or series of phases in the process of democratization the ultimate origin of which was probably not in capitalism but in the feudal beginnings of the culture of the West.

The Dissolution
of Political Economy

The transition from a productivist to a consumerist ideology among intellectuals on both sides of the Atlantic was evidenced first of all by the transformation of economic thought in the closing decades of the nineteenth century. At that time, the so-called "marginalist revolution" marked the dissolution of the classical bourgeois attitude toward political economy. I shall argue that the writings of such economists as Leon Walras in France, W. Stanley Jevons and Alfred Marshall in Great Britain, Karl Menger in Austria, and J. B. Clark in the United States, completed in the same generation more or less simultaneously, signaled the partial emergence of a new complex of values tied to the movement of Western culture *beyond* the productivist legacy of the Enlightenment. For Adam Smith, Ricardo, Mill, Marx, and even J. B. Say, production was the ultimate end of economic activity; for Jevons, Walras, Menger, Marshall, and Clark, consumption was the end. Where the classical political economists were practically (and for good reason) obsessed with finding the secret of increasing the "wealth of nations," the neoclassical or marginalist economists were more interested in distributing that wealth to the consumers. Accordingly, Jevons himself revealingly wrote that "every manufacturer knows and feels how closely he must anticipate the tastes and needs of his customers; his whole success depends upon it." He thus concluded that "the whole theory of Economy depends upon a correct theory of consumption." Mill and Marx had already begun to shift their interest in the direction of distribution without being able to transcend the productivist mentalité bequeathed to them from the Enlightenment. In contrast, the marginalists, whatever their faults, truly made a break with past ideologies.[1]

We have seen that the emergence of political economy as an autonomous science, as well as the related conception of property as the definitive realm of citizenship, was associated with the distinctively productivist ideology that first appeared in Western Europe and its North American colonies during the seventeenth and eighteenth centuries. The new science of economics seems to have emerged as a branch, or adjunct, to that *political science* concerned with the provisioning of the state and its army. In its protoeconomic or "mercantilist" phase, political economy was already concerned with production, if only for the ultimate end of the polity. During this same period, the mercantilist state was engaged in balancing the emerging power of the bourgeois strata of the commonality against the receding prestige of the upper two estates. In particular, the third order's stress on wealth remained subordinate to the aristocratic values of prayer and war during the Age of the Baroque.[2]

But by the middle of the eighteenth century, the idea of

1. W. Stanley Jevons, *The Theory of Political Economy* (London: Macmillan, 1871), p. 47; also see John Kenneth Galbraith, *The Affluent Society* (Boston: Houghton Mifflin, 1958), pp. 139–51. Stuart Chase, *Economy of Abundance*, is an early example of a work that postulates a new phase of Western culture beyond the protoindustrial culture of the nineteenth century.

2. For the dynamics of court society, see Norbert Elias, *The Court Society* (New York: Pantheon, 1983); Stoianovich presents an interesting discussion of the three orders in his article "Gender and Family"; see Louis Dumont, *From Mandeville to Marx: Genesis and Triumph of Economic Ideology* (Chicago: University of Chicago Press, 1977), pp. 5–6, 23–25, 33–38.

production was liberated from the ends of the state and became an end in itself. In both Great Britain and France, the wealth of nations began to replace the wealth of governments as the primary concern of social theorists. The emphasis remained, however, on production. Indeed, from the end of the seventeenth to the end of the nineteenth century, the particularly marked emphasis on the work ethic was concretized in the primacy of production in social theory from Locke to Marx. In classical economics production was glorified as the end of all human activity; consumption was merely a means to further production. This view represented a radical inversion of the older hierarchy of values in Western culture, which had associated work with the inferior third function of society while the functions of war and prayer were performed by the aristocracy. But in the seventeenth and eighteenth centuries, the gradual victory of the third Western "varna" was registered by the triumph of the ideology of production: it was work itself that became noble and sacred in the new mythology of social theory. In this context, the idea of good and evil was replaced by that of productive and unproductive. Classical economists thus found the secret of increasing wealth in the quasi-moral distinction between productive and unproductive consumption and judged human activity in terms of how it served the ends of production.[3]

The distinction between productive and unproductive consumption, like the closely related distinction between productive and unproductive labor, was one of the most ubiquitous characteristics of classical economics in the broadest sense of the term. Elements of the distinction appear in the work of Destutt de Tracy and Say, as well as that of Ricardo and Mill. The distinction is even pre-Smithian in origin, going back to the Physiocrats. Bound up with the general stigmatization of *rental* income, it is clearly connected to the revolt of

3. Dumont, *From Mandeville to Marx*, pp. 33–40.

the bourgeoisie against the pretensions of the aristocracy, a revolt that helped to shape the contours of productivist ideology in general.[4]

But after 1871, the ideological primacy of production was itself challenged by a still newer ideology of consumption. Elements of this new ideology were embodied in the writings of Jevons and his coworkers in the field of economics. The marginalists started from the assumption that human beings were first of all consumers. The distinction between productive and unproductive consumption, a distinction that Joseph Schumpeter in effect dismissed as a "dusty museum piece," tended to disappear when consumption became the end of all human activity.[5] Indeed, in the marginalist or "neoclassical" conception of economic life, it was production that became understood as somehow secondary, an unfortunate prerequisite for consumption. In other (appropriately Freudian) words, production was increasingly regarded as a "secondary" rather than a "primary" process. No longer the essence of life, it became a kind of detour. To be willing to undertake production, the marginalists argued, the consumer must be willing to postpone an immediate consumption (pleasure), but only in order to achieve a more probable consumption in the long run. "This power of anticipation," Jevons wrote, "must have a large influence in Economy." For Alfred Marshall, too, it was "human nature" generally to prefer immediate to delayed consumption. In this scheme, the capacity to undertake production develops in proportion to the capacity to envision future consumption and, thus, delay immediate

---

4. For a discussion of Destutt de Tracy's position on productive and unproductive classes, see Cheryl Welch's *Liberty and Utility: The French Ideologues and the Transformation of Liberalism* (New York: Columbia University Press, 1984) and my review of the same in *History Teacher* 19 (November 1985), 180–81.

5. See Joseph Schumpeter, *History of Economic Analysis* (New York: Oxford University Press, 1954), p. 628.

consumption in order to achieve a greater consumption in the future.[6]

Economists of the so-called Austrian school, centered in Freud's Vienna, postulated that in production, "a certain space of time, a certain production-period, elapses between the application of labor and the attainment of the finished product."[7] It is indeed, the redefinition of time that is a key indicator of the passing of productivist legacy of the Enlightenment. For Eugen von Böhm-Bawerk (1851–1914), a contemporary of Freud, production *was nothing but time.* In other words, not only was production displaced from its original primacy; it ceased to exist at all. In neoclassical thought, there was no production but only a ghostly substitute for production that took the form of an indirect or delayed consumption. Refraining from consumption over time appeared, at least to the Austrian school, enough to create more consumption since "there is interest without any production whatever, but never without time."[8]

By making "interest" the paradigm of the new conception of production, Böhm-Bawerk revealed that this conception was in fact the negation of production as previously understood. Production now appeared merely as an indirect or "round-about" form of consumption. For in contrast to the unending chain of expanding production envisioned by the classical economists, the neoclassical theorists gave production a definite—and finite—ending in consumption. Thus, unwittingly, they repealed the bourgeois law of progressive development implicit in the old classical conception of an ongoing and expanding production.[9]

6. Jevons, *Theory of Political Economy*, pp. 41–42; Alfred Marshall, *Principles of Economics* (London: Macmillan, 1907), pp. 120–21.

7. Eugen von Böhm-Bawerk, "The Positive Theory of Capital and Its Critics," *Quarterly Journal of Economics* 9 (January 1895), 123.

8. E. von Böhm-Bawerk, "The Positive Theory of Capital and Its Critics II," *Quarterly Journal of Economics* 9 (April 1895), 253.

9. For a more comprehensive examination of time and developmentalism in economic, biological, and social thought in the period from the late nineteenth century to the present day, see Birken, "Darwin and Gender."

I

The productivist ideology that informed "classical" or Enlightenment thought was, we have seen, a complex of several values. That ideology emphasized, on the one hand, the *productivity*, and, on the other hand, the *neediness*, of human beings. It was in this context that the British and Continental variants of premarginalist economics appeared, each accenting a different aspect of a common set of values. In the British variant, under which we would subsume the French Physiocratic school, commodity production (as well as the historical development it fueled) was understood as an open-ended process of expansion, a *perpetuum mobile* of increasing returns. To the Physiocrats, the soil was a source of a real and tangible surplus wealth. Grain reproduced endlessly in the works of Quesnay even as labor reproduced endlessly in the work of Adam Smith. Ricardo practically defined commodities by their characteristic of unlimited reproducibility.

In this British variant of early political economy, the reproducible commodity was paradigmatic and connected to the conception of production as a *real* process of value multiplication. Because products were understood to be reproducible, value was also seen as reproducible. The object of economics was to increase—produce—the wealth of nations. Implicit here was the faith that labor is the genuinely creative source of value, capable of overcoming nature in any contest. In the course of its expansion, the economy was supposed to embody an ever greater amount of real wealth, a wealth created by ceaseless labor. In Marx, who aggressively asserted the doctrine of labor-power's unlimited potential for growth, this faith in the creative power of labor reached its apogee.[10]

It was in the course of the nineteenth century that the idea

10. For an examination of Marx's productivist assumptions, see Baudrillard, *Mirror of Production*.

of reproducibility began to disintegrate. Ricardo had noted the existence of certain exceptional commodities, "the value of which is determined by their scarcity alone" because "no labor can increase the quantity of such goods."[11] He also perceived the scarce character of natural resources, which he contrasted with the unlimited reproducibility of human resources. But Ricardo refused to jettison the dominant Enlightenment paradigm of reproducibility, even though it could not explain the nature of scarcity. Instead, he upheld the productivist mentalité with its emphasis on a creative labor as the source of unlimited wealth.[12]

But after 1870, at the very time that Marx and Engels were developing the now old classical idea of the potentially unlimited increasing returns of unfettered labor, there appeared the elements of a new ideology of scarcity in which desiring individuals competed for scarce resources. Marginalism took the Ricardian exception and made it universal. Accordingly, an ecological conception of a universe governed by limited resources began to replace an economic conception of a universe open to improvement. By the last decade of the nineteenth century, a sterile desire had replaced a productive labor as the origin of value. By classical standards, there was actually no production at all in the neoclassical construct, merely the transformation of scarce resources into more or less desirable forms. Because the Ricardian exception, the scarce commodity, had become the rule, there was no longer any place for labor as a real process of *creating* new goods. Indeed, in the new paradigm, commodities themselves were not so much material goods as desired

---

11. David Ricardo, *The Works and Correspondence of David Ricardo*, ed. Piero Sraffa, vol I: *On the Principles of Political Economy and Taxation* (London: Cambridge University Press, 1982), p. 12. For Mill's summary of the labor theory of value, see J. S. Mill, *Principles of Political Economy* (New York: D. Appleton, 1895), p. 546.

12. For a discussion of the shift from the idea of productivity to that of scarcity, see David Levine, *Economic Studies: Contribution to the Critique of Economic Theory* (London: Routledge & Kegan Paul, 1977).

objects. Anything (material or not) that was desired was potentially a commodity.[13]

The emergence of this ecological conception should thus be associated with the shift in emphasis toward consumption in the late nineteenth century. From the perspective of the consumer, there can be no objective production but only the satisfaction or frustration of desire. The consumer recognizes production not as something real in itself but only as the deferral of consumption. In any case, from the point of view of the consumer, objects simply appear or do not appear; they are available or not available, however they are produced.[14]

In the Continental variant of early political economy, the issues were different. Continental theories emphasized the neediness of human beings. This was an important Enlightenment idea that also found echoes in the theories of Adam Smith and Marx. Precisely because it subordinated consumption to production, classical thought, both in Britain and on the Continent, tended to assume that needs were determined by the economy (productive order) as a whole on the basis of certain universal "species" requirements.[15]

In the British school, to be sure, this conception of need remained somewhat obscure because it was overshadowed by the emphasis on productivity and the labor theory of value. On the Continent, though, the Enlightenment conception of need took on a more definite form in the famous utility theory of value. From, say, 1750 to 1870 early economic thought conceived of utility in universal terms; water was supposed to have a greater utility than cake for *all* people. Hence, in constructing a theory of value based on utility or need, J. B. Say and his followers had to assume that those things (such as air, sunlight, and water) which

13. See ibid., pp. 175–202, 231–48.
14. Ibid., pp. 197–98.
15. A discussion of the Marxist conception of need is presented in John McMurtry, *The Structure of Marx's World-View* (Princeton: Princeton University Press, 1983), pp. 49–53.

were absolutely necessary for human life had value. Unfortunately, these Continental theorists were confronted with the empirical fact that, in some cases, these things are absolutely free. The inability of Say and his followers to explain why some necessary things were free, like Ricardo's inability to explain the price of exceptional scarce commodities, was a result of these economists' adherence, well into the nineteenth century, to the Englightenment vision of productive and needy human beings.[16]

The Continental or utility theory of value was based upon the premarginalist assumption of normal need, an assumption that led to many theoretical problems for early economists. This classical conception of need ignored the possibility of individual taste. But with the advent of marginalism, the idea of a universal set of needs disintegrated, to be replaced by a radically new emphasis on idiosyncratic desire. Only with the gradual recognition of the distinction between utility and marginal utility do we see the beginnings of a systematic ideology of individualistic desire. Whereas the concept of utility suggested a normative conception of need, the idea of marginal utility implied choice among an abundance of commodities. In other words, according to neoclassical theory, even if water has a greater (overall) utility than cake, one *more* unit of water may be of less (marginal) utility than one more unit of cake for a particular individual at a particular time. This situationalism, this radical relativization of value, is characteristic of the democratization implicit in a consumerist perspective. It was within this context that the individual's particular and unique wants became significant. The idea of need was

16. For an exposition of Say's theory of value, see J. B. Say, *A Treatise on Political Economy, or the Production, Distribution and Consumption of Wealth* (New York: Augustus Kelley, 1964), pp. 281, 359. In any case, Say seems completely unable to deal with the value of natural resources in a consistent way. For Walras's diagnosis of Say's problem, see Léon Walras, *Elements of Pure Economics*, trans. William Jaffé (Fairfield, Conn.: Augustus Kelley, 1977), pp. 201–4.

abolished, and the desire for different objects—cake and water, bread and perfume, sunlight and diamonds—was taken as equal and exchangeable desire. As this view developed in the late nineteenth century, it outmoded not only the idea of utility, but that of marginal utility as well, because the latter retained a trace of the former. Even the remnant of the idea of use which hid in the idea of marginal utility was outmoded because the completely random character of desire was now recognized. Economists increasingly understood that in their new science it was not that useful things were desired but that desired things were useful.[17]

II

Louis Dumont, following in the tradition of both Marxism and modernization theory, has delineated the emergence of what he calls the "economic category," a process only complete with the separation of production from morality in the seventeenth and eighteenth centuries. But we have seen that, during this period, consumption remained embedded in the quasi-moral distinction between productive and unproductive consumption explicit in classical economics. From this standpoint, the appearance of the neoclassical or marginalist paradigm indicated the emergence of what we might call the "psychosexual category," a process associated with the separation of consumption from morality. The marginalist revolution made consumption—the satisfaction of idiosyncratic desire—the end of all human activity and thus immune from moral scrutiny.[18]

Let me be more specific. In the classical period, "moral scrutiny" took the form of an endless search for a theory

17. Galbraith, *Affluent Society*, p. 147; H. J. Davenport, "Proposed Modifications in Austrian Theory and Terminology," *Quarterly Journal of Economics* 16 (May 1902), p. 356; Walras, *Elements*, p. 65.
18. See Dumont, *From Mandeville to Marx*.

of objective or "exchange" value that would regulate the economy as a *whole*. On the one hand, the English school emphasized the origin of value in social labor. On the other hand, the Continental school saw the origin of value in social need. But neither the British nor the Continental scheme of objective value was able to explain the full range of human behavior in regard to commodities. The labor theory could not explain the value of art works; the utility theory could not explain the lack of value of sunlight. Rather, these theories preserved a remnant of holism in the domain of consumption by positing what commodities *should* have value, a remnant that was incompatible with the individualistic elements of economics. It was this incompatibility that led to a contradiction between exchange value (whether based on social labor *or* social need) and idiosyncratic use value both in Great Britain and on the Continent. In contrast, the marginalists abolished the contradiction between exchange value and use value all at once by absorbing the first into the second, thus abolishing the last remnant of holism and morality governing the consumption of objects. In the last quarter of the nineteenth century, the marginalists thus replaced the contradictions of political economy with a coherent and suprisingly uniform theory of value. According to the new theory, value was neither the objective result of social labor nor of social need for products, but was simply attached to objects by the subjective desire of consumers.[19] In other words, value lost its social nature and took on a radically individual character. But when value disappeared as an objective social phenomenon, the self-determining character of the economic disappeared along with it. To evaluate value as subjective evaluation arising from idiosyncratic and arbitrary taste was to root the economic in the psychological.[20]

19. Hence there is a parallel between the emergence of subjective value in neoclassical economics and the moral relativism that tends to appear in psychology.

20. See Nina Shapiro, "The Revolutionary Character of Post-Keynesian Economics," *Journal of Economic Issues* 11 (September 1977), 560.

From the seventeenth to the nineteenth century, social theorists on both sides of the Atlantic tended to see society as a "reflex" of the economic, a vision that culminated in the universal theory of Marx. But by the end of the nineteenth century, the neoclassical conception reversed this hierarchy of values so that it was the economic that became the reflex of the psychological. In other words, the economic gradually ceased to understand itself as the autonomous center of social life and instead constituted itself simply as a means (technique) of satisfying radically idiosyncratic psychologies. In the process of becoming explicitly dependent on psychology, economic thought began to lose its preoccupation with self-renewal and growth. As long as production was the end, it was supposed to lead to more production, so that real growth was conceivable. But when the satisfaction of individual psychologies via consumption became the end of production, then the economic lost its self-sustaining quality and neither production nor growth was readily comprehensible anymore. Neoclassical thought thus explicitly granted what psychology was implicitly claiming at the same time: the primacy of the idiosyncratic consumer.

What is the significance of this new individualism based on desire? We have seen that the emergence of the productivist complex of values is associated with the triumph of the bourgeois strata of the third order over the upper two orders and the accompanying erosion of the remnants of feudalism in the seventeenth, eighteenth, and early nineteenth centuries. In the same way, the emergence of a consumerist complex of values must be associated with the erosion of the bourgeois order beginning after 1850. From the seventeenth to the nineteenth century, that order had been dominated by the ideal of *homo oeconomicus*, economic man, in the form of the citizen as property-owner and producer. The emergence of the economic and the accompanying separation of production from morality was conceptualized as the emancipation of the idiosyncratic *producer*. For social theorists from Locke to Marx, it was property-ownership, production, and labor that bestowed individuality. Indeed, even Marx justified socialism as the only vehicle for truly emancipating *homo oeconomicus*, the individual producer. It is safe to say, though, that if the classical conception of production was individualistic, its conception of desire was holistic. In the same way, although the economy was inhabited by individuals, women and children remained encased within the holistic realm of the family in classical thought.

In the classical conceptions of economics, then, desire was subordinated to need, understood as a holistic value. Individual *taste* was not recognized, at the theoretical level at least. In striking contrast, neoclassical thought possesses no concept of need. Instead, it takes idiosyncratic desire as a given. Desire, in the new conception, appears as an expression of individuals unfettered by social (productivist) determination. In the classical system, consumption was understood as need in part because it can be judged (as productive or unproductive) from the standpoint of productive society as a whole. In the neoclassical conception, however, desire is understood as the end of a "particular" individual who, as Dumont argues, "incarnates the whole of mankind."[21]

If the classical individual was liberated but also determined by his property, a determination that took place within the sphere of production, the neoclassical individual is liberated through and thus determined by his desire. But according to the neoclassical conception, desires, as Karl Menger noted, only "originate in the personality of the consumer."[22] Personality per se stands outside the boundaries of the classical sphere of the economy; from the point of view of those within this sphere, determination by desire is no determination at all. The neoclassical domain thus appears, according to economist Nina Shapiro, to be

21. Dumont, *Homo Hierarchicus*, p. 9.
22. Galbraith, *Affluent Society*, p. 144; Carl Menger, *Principles of Economics*, trans. James Dingwall and Bert Hoselitz (New York: New York University Press, 1976), p. 77.

"populated with free individuals whose very freedom precludes an explanation of their actions."[23] The historian of economic thought Rudolph Kaulla has indeed argued that "subjective value theories" preclude the formulation "of any general laws whatever" governing commodity exchange "except the psycho-physical . . . law of stimulus and sensation."[24] But this is simply to say that the neoclassical system made it impossible to explain economic behavior in terms of purely economic causation. The economic could no longer be explained from within, but only from without by psychological laws. These psychological laws, I intend to show, are precisely the laws developed by the sexologists.

What were the implications of the redefinition of individualism during the transition from classical to neoclassical theory? In the classical system, the active agents of society appeared to be the owners of commodities exchanged within the sphere of production. In contrast, the neoclassical system implied that desire was the only criterion for social agency. By portraying society as a collection of sovereign, desiring, perfectly competitive and idiosyncratic "ids," neoclassical theory extended the ideology of democracy further than it had been extended previously. Just how far that ideology was actually extended in the latter part of the nineteenth century will be the subject of the following chapters.

III

I have attempted to delineate the way marginalism repudiated several of the key productivist values associated with the emergence of political economy in the seventeenth and eighteenth centuries. We should perhaps ask ourselves, at this point, whether the neoclassical economics that

23. Shapiro, "Revolutionary Character," p. 560.

24. Rudolph Kaulla, *Theory of the Just Price: A Historical and Critical Study of the Problem of Economic Value*, trans. Robert Hogg (New York: Norton, 1940), p. 142.

appeared in the late nineteenth and early twentieth centuries is actually economics at all or whether it in fact constitutes a repudiation of economics. Certainly, an economics that has given up its own self-determination, its own moral structure, and its own unique dedication to increasing the wealth of nations appears to have repudiated its very *raison d'être*. But the question of the relationship between marginalism and earlier forms of economic theory is complicated by the tendency of the neoclassical economists to attempt a reconciliation with the classical ideology inherited from the preceding epoch. The process of repudiating the productivist complex of values was far from complete at the turn of the century; indeed, it is far from complete today. The tendency of new ideas to be absorbed into earlier ideological structures was of course operating here. Thus there was no question of the marginalists' trying to construct a pure science of consumption. Although they recognized (if only implicitly) the primacy of the psychological, they thought of themselves as economists and not psychologists. In other words, from the start marginalism attempted to reconcile itself with the earlier ideologies embodied by Smith and Say. This continuous attempt at reconciliation gave rise to a series of internal contradictions.[25] For example, because the entire conception of neoclassical economics was focused on the satisfaction of idiosyncratic desire, it should have been formally unimportant how or even whether the objects of desire are produced. The consumer, as I noted above, is interested only in whether objects are available, not in how they are made available. But in so far as neoclassical economists wanted to confront the economic world and the

25. I agree with Levine's brilliant analysis of the way in which marginalist economics abolishes the primacy of the economic and have attempted to incorporate his analysis into my larger historical framework. I am somewhat less sympathetic to Levine's effort to restore the primacy of the economic through a revival of classical conceptions of productivity and need within a modified post-Keynesian framework. From a historical perspective, any attempt at such a revival would be highly conservative and (perhaps) futile. But see Shapiro, "Revolutionary Character," pp. 541–55.

doctrine of political economy inherited from the preceding epoch, they were forced to confront objects as products. The task of marginalism was thus to explain production in terms of desire.[26]

The marginalists were thus confronted with the necessity of reconciling the constant or even increasing returns of production inherent in the Enlightenment universe with the decreasing returns characteristic of the fin-de-siècle conception of finite resources. A partial solution was found by generalizing the Ricardian conception of land as a nonreproducible or scarce means of production. Even if scarce objects were recognized as products, their means of production was scarce. The concept of production was itself transformed. Production came to be recognized as nothing more than a rearrangement of scarce objects into other objects more appropriate for consumption. Every product was simply a synthesis of scarce objects. Thus a type of artificial or synthetic production replaced the older conception of production as a real augmentation of wealth.[27] Production was now expressed only in terms of scarcity (the absence of productivity) and thus subordinated to the inevitable degeneration concretized in the idea of the "falling marginal product." The optimistic ideology of the Enlightenment was thus replaced by the pessimism characteristic of all those disciplines that embodied the consumerist complex of values.

The contradictions between the values of production and the values of desire implicit in neoclassical thought appear most dramatically in the work of Alfred Marshall, and this is true precisely because, more than any of his fellow marginalists, Marshall had a genuine respect for the classical economists. Accordingly, of all the neoclassical thinkers he formulated the most extensive account of the productive process. Within this account, Marshall introduced a new theory—

26. Levine, *Economic Studies*, pp. 175–222.

27. For a discussion of the marginalist concept of capital and value, see Nina Shapiro, "The Neo-Classical Concept of Capital," *Australian Economic Papers* 20 (June 1981).

that of the firm—to specify precisely how production must operate. Herein lay the contradiction: on the one hand, he grounded economic life in the idiosyncratic desire for scarce resources; on the other hand, he preserved some of the *values* of macroeconomics, of productivity and need, in his theory of the firm. The profit-maximizing firm was the Marshallian incarnation of the needy profit-maximizing individual of the classical system. In the fourth book and the thirteenth chapter of his *Principles of Economics*, Marshall provided an outline of the process of firm development and its relation to commodity production in which the increasing returns characteristic of the firm seem to replicate the growth pattern envisioned by classical political economists. In other words, in his theory of the firm, Marshall reintroduced the concept of growth and development which was missing from the postdevelopmentalist, neoclassical conception of the economy as a whole. In Marshall, the productivity of the firm seems to contradict the assumption of universal scarcity explicit in the neoclassical "ecological" perspective.[28]

Marshall's solution to the contradictions between the productivity implicit in the theory of the firm and the newer ecological assumptions of neoclassical ideology as a whole was to postulate a life history of the firm in which development (increasing returns) inevitably passes into degeneration (decreasing returns). For Marshall, the life history of the firm was a natural process, almost biological in character. A business, he believed, grows, reaches maturity, and then slips into old age and senility, thus precluding the possibility of any permanent tendency toward increasing returns to scale. Once again, the optimistic ideology of production was subordinated to the fin-de-siècle pessimism inherent in the concept of scarcity. Yet in so far as the marginalists attempted to take up at least some of the concerns of Smith,

28. Marshall, *Principles of Economics*, pp. 314–22; Levine, *Economic Studies*, pp. 248–74.

Ricardo, Marx, and Say, their new science resisted its own tendency to abandon the economic domain completely. The dissolution of political economy was not yet complete.[29]

29. Levine, *Economic Studies*, pp. 248–74; Piero Sraffa, "The Law of Returns under Competitive Conditions," *Economic Journal* 36 (December 1926).

CHAPTER TWO

The Emergence of Sexology

The emergence of sexology, at the very time when the marginalist paradigm was conquering the domain of political economy, is perhaps the most dramatic evidence of the shift from a productivist to a consumerist world view among intellectual circles on both sides of the Atlantic during the last quarter of the nineteenth century. If the marginalists were ready to concede that the entire economic system as they saw it was but a means to satisfy the desires of individual consumers, sexual scientists such as Krafft-Ebing and Freud were intent upon finding the laws that governed those desires. Because sexology, like marginalism, emerged during the transition from a productivist to a consumerist intellectual culture, we should expect these ideologies to exhibit similarities. It is in fact easy to show that they do. Sexual science shares many of the values evident in marginalism, especially the stress on scarcity and idiosyncratic consumption. Moreover, like marginalism, sexology exhibits the contradictory structure of an ideology simultaneously embodying both productivist and consumerist values.

Yet despite their tremendous similarities, similarities that deserve to be explored in detail, there are also tremendous differences in the roles played by these two sciences in the history of Western thought. It can be argued that neoclassical economics destroyed the natural law of property just when sexology was constructing a new natural law of desire. In other words, marginalism provided a dissolution at exactly the time that sexology was providing a solution to the problem of organizing consumption. It was precisely because they were searching for the laws determining desires that, just when marginalism had finally banished from political economy the moralism implicit in the distinction between productive and unproductive consumption, the sexologists attempted to reintroduce that moralism by positing a distinction between productive and unproductive desire. At the core of sexology was the ambition to, as Krafft-Ebing put it, "record the various psychopathological manifestations of sexual life in man and reduce them to their lawful conditions."[1] Thus, Havelock Ellis's principal aim was "to get into possession of the actual facts, and from the investigation of the facts . . . to ascertain what is normal and what is abnormal."[2] More central even than the "scientific" hunger for "facts" was the imperative that desire be reduced to a series of laws. In this sense, Krafft-Ebing, Havelock Ellis, and Freud were the real heirs to Smith, Ricardo, Say, and Marx, and the actual successor to the classical political economy of the eighteenth and nineteenth centuries was not marginalism but the sexology of the twentieth century. For sexual science, like classical economics, explicitly claimed to have discovered a self-determined order, even though the latter grounded that order in property while the former grounded order in the wider sphere of desire.

I

From Locke to Marx, liberal and radical thinkers alike had portrayed human beings as producers. But like neoclassical,

1. Richard von Krafft-Ebing, *Psychopathia Sexualis—with Especial Reference to the Antipathic Sexual Instinct: A Medico-Forensic Study*, trans. from the 12th German edition by Franklin Klaf (New York: Stein & Day, 1978), pp. xiii–xiv.
2. Ellis and Symonds, *Sexual Inversion*, p. ix.

sexological thought started with the assumption that individuals are first of all consumers. Just as marginalist thought sought to explain production from the perspective of consumption, sexology attempted to investigate reproduction from the point of view of desire. Yet, this process of investigation and explanation was also a process of covering up and explaining away. In a sense, there was no more reproduction in the work of Krafft-Ebing or Freud than there was genuine production in the work of Jevons or Walras. Just as the marginalists attempted to reduce production to a form of indirect consumption, sexologists tended to resolve "normal love" into a subtle form of indirect or "round-about" desire involving the deferral of immediate enjoyment.

In particular, sexual science closely associated desire with "spending," assuming an innate tendency to spend or discharge energy. Defining energy itself as scarce, sexologists believed that the act of consumption involved a depletion of nervous energy and its transformation into activity. In contrast, the building up of energy was associated with the deferral of consumption. For Havelock Ellis, a long period of abstinence "in which images, desires and ideals grow up within the mind" is the prerequisite for normal love.[3] Accordingly, Ellis emphasized the necessity of *tumescence* (the accumulation of energy or desire) as a precondition for *detumescence* (the discharge of energy or desire). Within this framework, Ellis distinguished between the immediate discharge of masturbation, the less immediate but still comparatively speedy discharge of so-called perversion, and the long-delayed discharge he believed inherent in normal or heterogenital love. In other words, normal love demands abstinence or time. In return, through time, it multiplies desire or value—a perfect parallel to Böhm-Bawerk's theory of production as round-about consumption through time.[4]

An understanding of the primacy of desire and discharge

3. Havelock Ellis, "The Analysis of the Sexual Impulse," *Alienist and Neurologist* 21 (April 1900), 262.

4. Robinson, *Modernization of Sex*, pp. 1–41; Ellis and Symonds, *Sexual Inversion*, p. 108.

in fin-de-siècle thought is vital to any analysis of Freudian theory. Consumerist values are already evident in Freud's preanalytic work, in particular his brilliant "Project for a Scientific Psychology" (1895), which constituted his last and greatest effort to derive psychology explicitly from neurophysiology. The "Project," interesting as it is in itself, is also a beautiful example of how consumerist values could be concretized in an enormously complicated theoretical construct. Freud's "Project" attempted to derive a complex range of mental phenomena from a few basic assumptions. He began with the postulate that the principal tendency of the nervous system is to divest itself of any excitation, assuming that discharge via the consumption of an object or/and the appropriate extinction of a desire is pleasure. Conversely, he believed that nervous energy or charge that cannot be discharged is pain. For Freud, the primary imperative toward discharge appeared as the tendency of the nervous system to discharge all energy, aiming for the "reduction . . . of tension to zero." In other words, he believed that the nervous system seeks to annihilate itself in death.[5]

But Freud immediately discovered a secondary or modifying principle; the exigencies of reality make immediate discharge impossible. From the start, the first reality of nervous life is that gratification must be postponed, and the first impediment to the discharge of nervous energy is the structure of the nervous system itself. In order for the nervous system to perform its function of discharge, that system must continue to exist as a form of congealed charge. That is, the day-to-day requirements of the nervous system require its continued existence. Ultimate discharge must thus be postponed even though it remains the eventual goal.[6]

5. Sigmund Freud, *The Origins of Psychoanalysis: Letters to Wilhelm Fliess, Drafts and Notes: 1887–1902*, ed. Marie Bonaparte, Anna Freud, Ernst Kris; trans. Eric Mosbacher and James Strachey (New York: Basic Books, 1954), pp. 356–58.
6. Ibid., pp. 358–63.

I will return to Freud's "Project" later, in a somewhat different context, but for now it may be useful to see how his original emphasis on consumer discharge was incorporated into psychoanalysis. Freud never gave up his fundamental assumption that this discharge was primary. Like Böhm-Bawerk and Marshall, he believed that the value of a deferred pleasure must be greater than that of an immediate pleasure if the primacy of pleasure is to be affirmed. So the principle of consumption became, for Freud, a "pleasure" principle. That principle, in turn, was modified by the exigencies of reproduction (under which Freud subsumes production), which constitute a secondary or "reality" principle. "Actually," Freud hastened to add, "the substitution of the reality principle for the pleasure principle implies no deposing of the pleasure principle, but only a safeguarding of it," because an uncertain immediate pleasure "is given up, but only in order to gain . . . an assured pleasure at a later time."[7]

In the language of the Austrian marginalists, we might say that for Freud the reality principle was a round-about form of the pleasure principle. In this context, the history of psychoanalysis as a theory is, in part, a history of how Freud continually transformed old pleasure principles into new reality principles. By 1905, for example, heterogenital love already functioned as the reality principle of the polymorphous sex drive. Freud's formulation of narcissism from 1910 to 1914, in turn, reduced all forms of object love, whether perverse or not, to a reality principle modifying the newly discovered primary tendency toward narcissism. Narcissism thus became the new pleasure principle, but unable to satisfy itself through itself, it invested in others as a round-about means of satisfying its own original desires. Self-desire would appear the most easily satisfied of desires;

7. Sigmund Freud, "Formulations on the Two Principles of Mental Functioning," *Standard Edition of the Complete Psychological Works of Sigmund Freud*, 23 vols. (London: Hogarth, 1953–1974), 12:23.

but the necessity of, in the real world, going through a period of dependency drives the human being out of what is in effect a Darwinian state of nature. The idiosyncratic consumer is thus "propelled" by self-interest into the social world. The human being is forced to invest in others as a round-about means of satisfying itself.[8]

In 1914, Freud noted that the "first auto-erotic sexual satisfactions are experienced in connection with vital functions which serve the purpose of self-preservation."[9] Gradually, desire for external objects, bound up with the task of self-preservation, emerges. Within this framework, Freud believed that the reality principle directs self-desire outward in a series of successive adjustments: after one's self, a similar individual (of the same sex), and eventually a fully complementary individual (of the opposite sex). Along a different axis, desire is directed outward to the mother, the father, and finally the social order itself. Freud thus implied that the choice of a more differentiated object of desire requires a higher level of investment (charge) in the same way that Ellis saw normal love as requiring a longer circuit of deferred desire.[10]

The withdrawal of desire from the self and its direction outward in order to facilitate the ultimate satisfaction of the self is simply one more form of round-about consumption or delayed discharge. But Freud modified even this vision when he constructed his final schedule of the instincts in 1920. There he extended desire to include death as well as life, thus finally realizing in psychoanalysis the titanic vision of life and death he first outlined in the "Project." In a sense, life itself, life embracing all desire including narcissism, becomes the ultimate reality principle modifying the

---

8. Sigmund Freud, "On Narcissism: An Introduction," *Standard Edition*, vol. 14.

9. Ibid., p. 87.

10. Ibid., pp. 100–102; see Jean Laplanche and Jean-Baptiste Pontalis, *The Language of Psychoanalysis*, trans. Donald Nicholson-Smith (London: Hogarth, 1973), s.v. "economic," "narcissism."

primary desire for total discharge. If death was the opposite of desire, it was also the ultimate desire.[11]

II

In sexology, the desire of the consumer—or more accurately the desire in the consumer—was subordinated to what psychoanalysis calls an "economic" principle. However, this principle was economic only in a marginalist sense, rather than in a Smithian or Marxian sense. Libido was no magical self-reproducing substance like Marxian labor, but a scarce natural resource. In the latter decades of the nineteenth century, sex energy was understood as a nonreproducible substance. Just as there was no production but only the recombination of scarce resources in the neoclassical theories of economics, there was only the recombination and transformation of scarce energies in sexology. Like the marginalists, the sexologists embraced an "ecological" rather than an "economic" principle. And it was precisely in this context that sexual science hypothesized the possibility of what we might call libidinal transformations. Sexual energy, it was widely believed, might be diverted from one region of the body to another, from one object to another; this was the basis for the so-called hydraulic character of psychoanalytic thought. Freud regarded libido as a kind of fluid energy that could be shunted, dammed up, or diverted. Of course, this fluid energy tended to discharge via the shortest path available. In addition, when dammed up so that discharge was permanently delayed, sexual energy appeared to transform itself into symptoms. Freud's theory of illness, as it emerged in the last decade of the nineteenth century, followed the general tendency in psychosexual theorizing by assuming an "ecology" of desire.

11. See Siegfried Bernfield and Sergei Feitelberg, "The Principle of Entropy and the Death Instinct," *International Journal of Psychoanalysis* 12 (1931), 62–63, 78–79.

Such theorizing incorporated a generous amount of pessimism in its structural baggage. From the ecological perspective, the objects of desire appeared to be as scarce as the desire directed toward them. One might well go further and observe that in this view the sexual object is the scarce object par excellence. There is a poignancy in desire precisely because its object is formally nonreproducible. In this sense, the extension of the idea of scarcity in the course of the nineteenth century represented a sexualization of the economic more than a mercantilization of the sexual. The productivist ideology of the Enlightenment had relegated scarce objects, the Ricardian exceptions, and other curiosities of the "natural world," to the periphery of social theory; the establishment of a consumerist ideology involved the generalization of the idea of scarcity. In this context, the object of sexual desire is the prototypic scarce object. It is either available or not; certainly it is not a commodity with which a triumphant labor can supply us. From the sexological perspective, like that of the marginalists, however, *all* objects are scarce, thus implying the disappearance of labor as a factor in creating *any* object.[12]

From the sexological point of view, economic objects represent only a part of the world of objects desired by the consuming individual, and hardly the most significant part; sexual objects are more interesting. It may well be argued, however, that in psychoanalysis, *all* desired objects are ultimately sexual objects since "sex" is synonomous with "desire" in general. Moreover, if we examine the fundamental assumptions of sexology, and especially psychoanalysis, we should find that these assumptions are similar to those underlying marginalist economics. In particular, we may speak of a general law of "falling marginal utility" applying to all desired objects and not merely economic objects. According to this law, which, I would argue, was an underlying assumption of psychoanalysis as well as of marginalist

12. See Levine, *Economic Studies*, passim.

economics, the number of objects of desire is potentially unlimited but desire directed toward any one object soon falls off because desire is itself scarce. In the context of the hierarchy of wants distinguishing normal from perverse desire, the concept of falling marginal utility would imply that if more pressing (normal) desires are satiated, less pressing (perverted) desires will come to the fore. In the later decades of the nineteenth century, the generalization of the ecological principle and its corollary of diminishing returns appeared in the common argument that linked high civilization to overstimulation (neurasthenia). High civilization thus appeared to embody a tendency toward the degeneration and disintegration of the heterogenital primacy. Under conditions of economic overstimulation, it was believed, marginal land was put into cultivation. Under analogous conditions of sexual overstimulation, it was equally believed, marginal sexualities are cultivated.[13]

But a strange thing happened. At first, normal sexuality or heterogenitality appeared a normal need. But the spread of the marginalist ecological perspective in the later nineteenth century tended to undermine this concept of normality that it was actually attempting to preserve. Under conditions of overstimulation, it had to be admitted, the desire (marginal utility) for a perverted sexual object might be greater than the desire (marginal utility) for a normal sexual object. By degrees, the development of this idea perforce encouraged the tendency to make various forms of normal and abnormal sexuality equivalent and exchangeable desires, thus abolishing the distinction between the normal and the abnormal.

III

Better to understand the emergence of the conception of idiosyncratic desire, and how sexology simultaneously strug-

13. See George Beard, *Sexual Neurasthenia* (New York: Arno, rpt., 1972), passim.

gled against and furthered the development of that concept, one must recognize that just as classical political economy postulated a society in which individual property owners freely entered into economic relations with each other, sexology conceived of a wider society in which idiosyncratic consumers freely entered into erotic relations with each other.[14] Only with the advent of the idea of the consuming individual, no longer defined by and thus no longer subject to the law of the economic sphere, was it necessary to subjugate that individual to the larger sphere delineated by sexology. As economic man realized his freedom only by submitting to the law of the market, so psychological man and woman realize their freedom only by submitting to the law of the sexual market.

In other words, sexology simultaneously discovered and attempted to regulate the idiosyncratic consumer. On the one hand, sexual science emphasized the multiplicity of individual preferences and thus the uniqueness of each person's "consumption bundle" or "case." So the American physician Frank Lydston argued, around 1890, that "as we may have variations of physical form and of mental attributes, in general, so we may have variations and perversions . . . of sexual affinity."[15] On the other hand, the sexologists attempted to subjugate these varied desires to an immanent law of sex.

If, as Dumont argues, the individual "incarnates the whole of mankind," then the appearance of the idea of the consuming individual is signaled by the emergence of the idea that each person is capable of all possible desires, an idea concretized in Freud's conceptualization of the "polymorphous perverse." I am arguing that the appearance of the consumer world view followed the emergence of a

14. In this sense, the following analysis in this and succeeding chapters treats the "sexonomic" order in a way analogous to the manner in which Dumont, Karl Polanyi, and Nikolai Bukharin have treated the "economic order."

15. Frank Lydston, "Sexual Perversion, Satyriasis and Nymphomania," *Medical and Surgical Reporter* 61 (1889), 255.

conviction, increasingly widespread, that each individual begins with a polymorphous potential to desire everything. Only in the course of their lives do these individuals become erotic specialists exhibiting particular compounds of desire or "sexualities." Now, classical economics had always started with the assumption of the polymorphous *producer* who in the course of his life becomes a specialist in the economy. Sexology expressed the same conviction about the domain of the consumer, starting with the assumption of the polymorphous desiring individual who eventually specializes in particular tastes. Through specialization, individuals starting out the same fulfill their individuality. Individuality was thus expressed through production in classical thought, and through desire in the more recently constructed ideology of the sexologists.[16]

More specifically, the emancipation of what I have chosen to call the "psychosexual" category was signaled by the dissolution of the holistic concept of need and the consequent emergence of the radically individualistic concept of desire among intellectual circles in the later decades of the nineteenth century. Thus, from its inception, sexology in its different forms represented (even as it struggled against) the dissolution of heterogenitality as a universal "species need" in favor of the emancipation of idiosyncratic desire in the form of "fetishes."

That is to say, until the last quarter of the nineteenth century, holistic values continued to shape the definition of consumption as a process of the satisfaction of universal human needs. Under these circumstances nothing appeared more natural and universal than heterogenital coitus and nothing more unnatural and idiosyncratic than nonprocreative sexuality. But sexology was to dissolve these distinctions even as it desperately sought to uphold them, by understanding desire in its radically idiosyncratic form as "fetishes" or "perversions." For sexology, desire in the form

16. See Dumont, *Homo Hierarchicus*.

of fetishes or perversions began to appear the most natural and immediate; that is, it seemed the most fundamental expression of the autonomous consumer. Conversely, heterogenitality began to be understood only as a synthesis of impulses, a synthetic and thus unnatural construct. The French psychologist Alfred Binet, for example, postulated that normal love is that form of love which is nobler than all other forms simply because it is the sum of all the other forms. In 1887, in an article published in the *Revue Philosophique*, Binet argued that "normal love appears to us now as the result of a complex fetishism. . . . one could say that in normal love the fetishism is polytheistic: it results not from one excitement, but a myriad of excitements: it is a symphony." In his *Psychopathia Sexualis*, Krafft-Ebing expressed a similar view, and Charles Féré, a French physician attached to the Bicêtre, echoed this opinion, holding that in "normal love all the elements of a person seem to combine in attracting." In psychoanalysis, Freud reproduced these ideas in his contention that normal love or coitus was a complex synthesis of "component instincts" which emerges at puberty when "a new sexual aim appears and all the component instincts combine to attain it."[17]

In contrast to the solution of normal love, abnormal love was increasingly understood as a dissolution of sex. Sexologists stigmatized the perverse as dissolute because in it the various elements (fetishes) that combined in normal love appeared to take on lives of their own as idiosyncratic preferences. Ironically, in this sense, the very appearance of sexology as a science of idiosyncratic preferences bore witness to the dissolution of sex. In fact, however, this dissolution was only the dissolution of the older conception

---

17. Alfred Binet, "Le fétichisme dans l'amour," *Revue Philosophique* 24 (1887), 274, my translation; Krafft-Ebing, *Psychopathia Sexualis*, pp. 11–15; Charles Féré, *The Sexual Instinct: Its Evolution and Dissolution*, trans. Henry Blanchamp (London: The University Press, 1900), pp. 157–58; Sigmund Freud, *Three Essays on the Theory of Sexuality*, trans. James Strachey (New York: Basic, 1975), p. 73.

of sex as heterogenitality in favor of a new and wider definition of sex as desire, a desire most perfectly realized in
the psychoanalytic canon. In the process of redefinition,
though, coitus, once the simplest of needs, became the most
complex of desires, while idiosyncratic desire, once the most
unnatural phenomenon, became the most natural manifestation of the human being. Caught in its own contradictory
structure, suspended between a productivist culture of procreation and a consumerist culture of polymorphous perversion, sexology was obsessed with building the anarchic sexuality of the fetish back up into heterogenitality.

IV

In sexology, the tendency toward the dissolution of the
idea of need was paralleled by a tendency toward the dissolution of sex distinctions. From the seventeenth to the
nineteenth century, social theorists on both sides of the
Atlantic restricted the field of social agency to the masculine
domain of property, excluding from the realm of citizenship
the feminine domain of familial life. This dichotimization
between masculinity and femininity was no transhistorical
phenomenon, but rather one specifically connected to the
emergence of the bourgeoisie in the seventeenth and eighteenth centuries. Linda Nicholson, in particular, has stressed
that both state and family emerged during the transition to
capitalism. Along these lines, Traian Stoianovich has suggested that during the period from 1750 to 1850 the assertion
of the third estate against the upper two (noble and clerical)
estates should be associated with a process of "virilization."
According to Stoianovich, after, say, 1750 the ideology of the
three functions of priests, warriors, and commoners was
replaced by a system of two functions, one masculine and
one feminine. It happened, Stoianovich claims, when the
emancipated third function, led by the bourgeoisie and heretofore connected to the lowly function of production and

reproduction, constituted itself as the nation. At that time, it reorganized itself into a new duality in which masculine production was opposed to feminine reproduction. In effect, Stoianovich argues, the bourgeois ideologists accentuated the association of masculinity with production and femininity with reproduction as a form of masculine protest against the formerly servile and thus feminine status of the third estate. Although Stoianovich limits his study to France, the process of virilization may have been even more dramatic elsewhere in the West, especially in the United States which, to annex the American historian Louis Harz to Stoianovich, was "born" in the bourgeois-masculine epoch. That epoch, Stoianovich asserts, extended from about 1750 to 1860, after which it was reversed by the effects of mass production and consumerism.[18]

From the perspective I am developing, it can be argued that just as classical economics discovered labor as the underlying unity of the masculine sphere of property, so sexology discovered desire as the unity underlying *both* sexes. Although this sexless desire was *implicit* in the Darwinian contribution, it is only in the latter part of the nineteenth century that the "virilized" tendency to accentuate sex distinctions began to be reversed so that the idea of *sexuality* as something common to both sexes could gain ground.[19] The recognition of a "third sex," "sexual intermediates," and "intersexes" reduced the "normal male" and the "normal female" to two points on a sexual continuum. To adopt Dumont's expression once again, the consuming individual "incarnates" both male and female. Only in the course of their lives do individuals take on particular and idiosyncratic positions on the sexual continuum. For example, in Krafft-Ebing's account of *eviration* and *defemination*

18. Linda Nicholson, *Gender and History: The Limits of Social Theory in the Age of the Family* (New York: Columbia University Press, 1986); Stoianovich, "Gender and Family."

19. For an example of this post-Darwinian ideology, see Colin Scott, "Sex and Art," *American Journal of Psychology* 7 (January 1896), 161.

the same individuals might exhibit, in the course of their lives, two different sexualities.[20] Again, the discovery of the human being's *bisexuality*, like the discovery of the *id*, simply revealed a new conception of the individual's polymorphous potential as a consumer.

But the very ideology that grasped the genderless character of the consumer in all its radicality could not help trying to reaffirm the bourgeois polarity of the sexes. Sexology simultaneously implied the abolition of gender and remained obsessed with gender. In 1896, the American psychologist Colin Scott specified a "primary law of courting" in which "the male is physically active, but non-reflective, the female is passive, but imaginatively attentive to the states of the excited male." Consequently, the woman sees herself through the eyes of the man, desiring herself because she desires what the male desires. The same year that Scott published his article "Sex and Art," Havelock Ellis described the "tendency which is sometimes found, more especially perhaps in women, for the sexual emotions to be absorbed, and often entirely lost, in self-admiration." Ellis called this a "Narcissus-like" phenomenon. Of course, these formulations anticipated by some years the psychoanalytic dichotimization of the sexes linking narcissistic desire to females and anaclitic desire to males.[21]

The contradictions of sexology specifically expressed themselves in the ambiguous position of the female which prevailed in that science. For example, Scott conceived of the male as catabolic (tissue destroying) and the female as anabolic (tissue conserving). In this scheme, which Scott held in common with many other late-nineteenth-century scientists, the male's unambiguous position as a consuming citizen was symbolized by a catabolic process associated with the discharge of energy. In contrast, the anabolic

20. See Krafft-Ebing, *Psychopathia Sexualis*, pp. 195–96.
21. Scott, "Sex and Art," p. 207; Havelock Ellis, "Auto-Erotism: A Psychological Study," *Alienist and Neurologist* 19 (January 1898), 280; Freud, "On Narcissism."

character of the woman seemed to exclude her (again!) from the realm of consumer and citizen. But Scott also noted that erotic activity (consumption) "of any kind in both male and female represents a catabolic crisis," thus revealing the transsexual nature of the contractual model and the individuals who partake in it. In the same manner, Freud argued that "libido is invariably and necessarily of a masculine nature, whether it occurs in men or in women." In formulating his concept of penis-envy, Freud simultaneously treated women as individuals who can compete with and envy men in the same individualistic sphere of action, and specified that this envy is invariably directed toward the masculine.[22]

What are we to make of all this? It would seem that a genderless and a gendered conception of human life dwell together in the same ideology. Women were simultaneously included in and excluded from the realm of consumption and citizenship. One solution to this contradiction was to posit femininity as a "round-about" process of consumption. In his study of criminology, Havelock Ellis thus suggested that criminality (like libido) is both masculine and genderless. If the female criminal, Ellis believed, "wants a crime committed, she can usually find a man to do it for her." In other words, sexology took part in a general intellectual culture in which the inherited bourgeois distinctions between sexes were breaking down. Sexology increasingly understood the woman as classical political economy once understood the worker: as both active and passive. In courting, Colin Scott argued, the woman simultaneously advances and retreats, thus demonstrating "two contradictory impulses." Rather, it was sexology that exhibited the contradictory impulses, upholding species needs and gender on the one hand and idiosyncratic desire and genderlessness on the other. Formed during a phase in our intellec-

---

22. Scott, "Sex and Art," p. 157; Freud, *Three Essays*, p. 85. For a different view of penis-envy, see Illich, *Gender*.

tual history when the "woman question" was debated in an increasingly serious manner, sexology juxtaposed the second-rate status of women inherited from the Enlightenment with a newer transsexual ideal, the pre-Darwinian with the post-Darwinian. On the one hand, women were excluded from the "sexonomy" as a legacy of the productivist past; on the other hand they were included in token of the consumerist future.[23]

23. Scott, "Sex and Art," p. 169; Havelock Ellis, *The Criminal* (London: Walter Scott, 1897), p. 263. *The Criminal*, originally published in 1890, was one of Ellis's earliest works, antedating even the first edition of *Man and Woman*, and should be read before one turns to his sexological writings.

CHAPTER THREE

Evolution and Devolution

In addition to the erosion of gender and the disintegration of the idea of species needs, the passing of bourgeois culture has been accompanied by the dissolution of the concept of what Donald Lowe calls "development-in-time."[1] Enlightenment culture was drunk with the wine of developmentalism. For that culture, the new ideal of progress revealed itself as a process of increasing returns in production and a succession of modes of production in history. Thinkers as diverse as Turgot in France and Adam Smith in Britain described the appearance, in order, of a hunting stage, a pastoral stage, an agricultural stage, and a commercial stage of civilization.[2] Hegel, elaborating what was perhaps the most abstract form of this philosophy, described world history as "nothing but the development of the idea of Freedom."[3] According to Hegel, this idea progressively developed in the Oriental (Chinese, Indian, and Iranian), Greek, and Roman "worlds," culminating in the universal freedom of Germanic or Western civilization.[4] This developmentalist thought was

1. Lowe, *History of Bourgeois Perception*, pp. 1–16, 35–58.
2. See Ronald Meek, *Smith, Marx and After* (London: Chapman & Hall, 1977), pp. 18–34.
3. G. W. F. Hegel, *Philosophy of History* (New York: Dover, 1956), p. 456.
4. Ibid., p. 104.

always characterized by the tendency to evaluate all the civilizations in the world in terms of the Western criteria of progress, thus reducing all other cultures to primitive forms of Western culture and elevating that culture to the position of the end or *telos* of history. In other words, the Occidental experience of change and historical instability was universalized. Even Marx, in spite of his fleeting notions of an "Asiatic" or "slave" mode of production, took the dialectic movement characteristic of Western history since the Middle Ages as the universal law of historical motion.[5]

During the course of the nineteenth century, the scope of this careless developmentalism was gradually broadened to include nature as well as society. It was J. B. P. A. Lamarck (1744–1829) who, according to none other than Charles Darwin, "first did the eminent service of arousing attention to the probability of all change in the organic . . . world being the result of law." In Lamarck's account of evolution not only was there a progressive development of lower species into higher species, but "in order to account for the existence at the present day of simple productions," he believed that these were "now spontaneously generated." Lamarck's approach was thus in accord with the widespread developmentalist assumptions of classical culture and classical political economy.[6]

In contrast, the Darwinian scheme of random variation and natural selection was more ambivalent toward the idea of progress, marking in some ways a break with that idea. Darwin believed that random environmental conditions selected among chance variations. Since environments were themselves generated randomly, the entire Darwinian evolutionary mechanism depended on an unpredictable set of factors. *Formally*, such a mechanism banished teleology and

5. For Marx on modes of production outside the West, see Karl Marx, *Pre-Capitalist Economic Formations*, ed. Eric Hobsbawm, trans. Jack Cohen (New York: International Publishers, 1964).

6. Charles Darwin, *The Origin of Species by Means of Natural Selection* (New York: Penguin, 1981), p. 54.

thus progress from the intellectual universe. Moreover, Darwin thought that species became more "perfected" only in the sense that they became adapted to their respective environments. Implicitly, then, the Darwinian vision was one in which species came into being and passed away into oblivion without pattern or purpose. Darwin furthered the democratization of the species.[7]

But this democratic aspect of Darwinian thought, an aspect that threatened to banish development-in-time from intellectual life, was always in conflict with the developmentalist aspect of evolutionary theory inherited from Lamarck. In the end, Darwin was too much a part of his own age to break with developmentalism completely. He even came to accentuate the Lamarckian aspects of his theory in order to explain evolutionary theory better to a skeptical world. That world was, at any rate, more likely to accept a doctrine that would uphold rather than undercut the claims to world domination made by adult, white, middle-class European males. Thus, Darwin could not help at times identifying evolution with progress. Indeed, he postulated a general law linking progress to differentiation by arguing that the physiological "division" of labor constitutes an absolute advantage.[8] However much it contradicted his more radical discoveries about nature, he could not help believing that there was a kind of social progress culminating in the "western nations of Europe, who now so immeasurably surpass their former savage progenitors, and stand at the summit of civilization."[9]

Modified by Darwin himself, the democratic elements of his theory were further modified by the prevailing developmentalist intellectual climate. In the late nineteenth century, Darwin's theory of evolution was partially reabsorbed into

7. Ibid., passim.

8. See Charles Darwin, *On the Origin of Species* (Cambridge: Harvard University Press, 1964), pp. 93–94.

9. Darwin, *The Descent of Man, and Selection in Relation to Sex*, Book I, p. 178.

the bourgeois ideology of development-in-time. Yet the newer elements could not be totally extirpated. So fin-de-siècle evolutionary theory was in fact bedeviled by a fundamental contradiction, and sexology, shaped by evolutionary theory, inherited that internal contradiction. In the science of sex, a productivist developmentalism warred with a consumerist tendency to banish developmentalism.[10]

I

In the latter part of the nineteenth century, evolutionary theory, with all its contradictions, permeated the world of medicine. Darwin himself had prophesied that "psychology" would "be based on a new foundation, that of the necessary acquisition of each mental power and capacity by gradation."[11] As Frank Sulloway's important study of Freud suggests, Darwin was the first real sexologist and the emergence of sexology began with the publication of *The Descent of Man, and Selection in Relation to Sex* in 1871. It was Darwin in fact who was the first to postulate a primary tendency toward consumption, modified by a secondary tendency toward the deferral of consumption. For Darwin, this primary tendency expressed itself as the hunger that fueled the competition for resources and environmental niches. Darwin began with the assumption that individuals were fundamentally consumers. By tracing the pedigree of the human species, he revealed that the fundamental character of the individual was radically different from that postulated by classical thought. But his picture of natural selection was complicated by his conception of sexual selection; his notion of the radically individualistic hungry consumer was modi-

10. For an overall (but alternative) discussion of Darwinism and progress, see Anthony Leeds, "Darwinism and 'Darwinian' Evolutionism in the Study of Society and Culture," in Thomas Glick, ed., *The Comparative Reception of Darwinism* (Austin: University of Texas Press, 1972), pp. 437–85.

11. Darwin, *Origin of Species*, p. 488.

fied by his vision of the cooperative lover. Darwin's theory of sexual selection actually imposed upon the human being a secondary principle; hunger motivated individuals to compete, but love motivated them to wait.

In this section, I shall argue that the Darwinian doctrine of sexual selection is in some sense an intellectual ancestor of the Freudian conception of the reality principle. Following Darwin, sexologists in the last quarter of the nineteenth century conceived of the modification of lust by love, of egotism by altruism, as a slow "evolutionary" process extending over eons. In 1891, the American alienist James Kiernan (1852–1923), director of a Chicago asylum, hypothesized that "from . . . the utmost expression of egotism," primeval organic hunger, "has developed a secondary 'ego,' which inhibits explosive manifestations of egotism." In France, Féré argued in a similar manner that the instincts of individual self-preservation were eventually modified by the social instincts, sexual desire being initially associated with the former and only by degrees with the latter.[12]

Around 1898, Albert Moll (1862–1939) divided human desire into two "component instincts": the primeval instinct to discharge, which he called "detumescence," and the more recently evolved instinct to seek out another individual, which he called "contrectation." The first instinct was fundamentally individualistic, the second social. Moll theorized that primeval organisms that reproduce asexually by fission or budding possess only the instinct of detumescence, but the later organisms that reproduce by conjugation or sex have acquired the instinct of contrectation as well. In sexually reproducing animals, then, the instinct of detumescence is insufficient to guarantee reproduction. It is supplemented, however, by the instinct of contrectation, which,

12. Sulloway, *Freud: Biologist of the Mind*, provides an exhaustive if not very systematic discussion of sexology from Darwin to Freud. See in particular the chapter on sexology and the comprehensive bibliography, pp. 290–96. James Kiernan, "Psychological Aspects of the Sexual Appetite," *Alienist and Neurologist* 12 (1891), 217; Féré, *Sexual Instinct*, pp. 8–9.

predicated on attention to an external object, more closely resembles what we know as love. For Moll, love itself is thus a by-product of the evolution of sex.[13]

The sexologists were committed to explaining how this evolution of sex happened. Kiernan saw the answer in "the tendency of a complex mental state to inhibit a simple explosive tendency." In explaining how a more "advanced" (round-about) form of consumption may arise from and yet inhibit a more "primitive," (direct) one, Kiernan anticipated Freud's conception of the reality principle. And like Freud, Kiernan employed a subtle neo-Lamarckian framework to translate his reality principles into secondary pleasure principles; that is, to translate production (the deferral of consumption) into instinctive enjoyment (consumption). For Kiernan, love came into being when "attempts to please the cause of sexual pleasure, in themselves finally pleased without the presence of the cause." In the same way, by successive and gradual modifications, by gradations, evolution could build up the sexual sociability of contrectation from the narcissistic individuality of detumescence.[14]

Havelock Ellis and Albert Moll may have been the two most important figures in sexology before 1910. Like Moll, Ellis emphasized the developmental character of sexuality. In the course of evolution, he argued, the process of tumescence or deferral of discharge became increasingly prolonged. Ellis believed that as courting became increasingly delayed in the higher species, the ultimate discharge became increasingly powerful. He associated the development of sexual reproduction with the evolution of an immense accumulation of charge, and thus correspondingly powerful discharges during orgasm. Under these circumstances, though, he believed that higher organisms were tempted not to wait but to discharge more or less immediately by

13. Albert Moll, *Libido Sexualis: Studies in the Psychosexual Laws of Love Verified by Clinical Case Histories*, trans. David Berger (New York: American Ethnological Press, 1933), pp. 53, 123.

14. Kiernan, "Psychological Aspects," p. 191.

means of masturbatory or perverse action outside the realm of courtship. In this case, Ellis argued, the accumulated charge and the corresponding discharge would be comparatively weak and would represent a regression back to an earlier level of erotic life.[15] For Ellis, then, it was the exigencies of courtship (sexual selection) that modified the original idiosyncratic desire.

As well as putting forth the theory of how the instincts differentiated, sexologists also explained how the so-called erotogenic or erogenous zones emerged. Evolutionary theory suggested that in the primeval organism desire was equally distributed throughout the protoplasm. Just as the instinct of desire was once fused with that of hunger, the zone of reproduction was once fused with the zone of digestion. Indeed, sexologists and other students of evolution assumed a lack of differentiation as the central characteristic of "primitiveness." In the course of evolution, it was widely argued, specialization increased so that the zones of reproduction, ingestion, and defecation were gradually separated. With the sexually reproducing animals, specifically sexual organs developed, though secondary erotic zones in particular regions of the body remained as a legacy fron an earlier epoch.[16]

From the beginning, Freud's training in biology and neurology made him sensitive to these doctrines. Within the nervous system, he believed, there had also been a process of differentiation. In the "Project," the consumerist characteristics of which I have already emphasized, Freud postulated that there might be relatively permeable nerve cells that permitted discharge as well as relatively impermeable nerve cells that resisted it. Freud identified the first group of cells as the Φ system, located in the "grey matter of the spinal cord" and engaged in perception, and the second

---

15. Ellis, "Analysis of the Sexual Impulse," pp. 247–63.
16. See Krafft-Ebing, *Psychopathia Sexualis*, pp. 24–25; Scott, "Sex and Art," p. 155.

group of cells as the Ψ system, located in the "grey matter of the brain" and engaged in receiving internal stimuli and memories. The memory capacity of the second system, Freud believed, was a function of the cells', impermeability, or, rather, their transient impermeability. For these cells could be worn down; charge, having flowed through them, could more easily flow through them again because the resistance or impermeability was lessened. In this way, Freud could explain memory itself as an actual physical legacy of the previous erosion of Ψ cells. In the process of erosion, these cells became increasingly like their Φ sisters. What is important is that Freud thought the latter cells were more fundamental, more primitive. Because he believed that the original tendency of organic matter was to discharge, he could only hold that cells comparatively resistant to discharge must be more recent. For this very reason, he localized the system of Φ cells in the comparatively archaic spinal region. In contrast, the Ψ system is organized in the more recently "acquired" brain.[17]

Building on the ideas expressed in the "Project," Freud hypothesized that evolution tended to produce organisms that are increasingly resistant to discharge. Thus, the regions of easy discharge became ever more restricted as the "higher" organisms emerged. In those organisms, these regions were limited to particular "erotogenic" zones, associated with specific erotic "aims." Among human beings, "aims" are in turn modified by the exigencies of "object-love." That is to say, for Freud, the satisfaction of an erotic aim, even though it takes the path of least resistance in the discharge of nervous energy (detumescence), may be complicated by the exigencies of finding a suitable sexual object (contrection). After 1910, he formulated narcissism as still another example of the self-preservation instinct that could be traced back to the primeval consuming, undifferentiated "hunger." Here, too, psychoanalysts posit that the idiosyn-

---

17. Freud, *Origins of Psychoanalysis*, pp. 359–60.

cratic consumption principle that they call narcissism was modified by the necessities of pleasing an external or social object of love for the eventual purpose of reproduction.

II

During the last quarter of the nineteenth century, much was written in medical circles about "degeneration." Though as early as 1897, Havelock Ellis believed that the term had become virtually meaningless because it was used so imprecisely, its vague meaning still supplies the clues we need to understand its place in late-nineteenth-century thought. In his *Sexual Inversion*, Ellis offers us the widest possible definition of *degenerate* as "fallen away from the genus."[18] Yet all the more somber fin-de-siècle definitions of *degenerate* and *degeneration* can be related to Ellis's literal explanation. Implicitly, degeneration is equivalent to variation. That is, Darwin's great contribution to and also his break with bourgeois culture lay in his recognition of variation among and thus the possession of idiosyncratic characteristics by organisms. In this sense. Darwinism was the last and greatest ideology of individualism. But by putting variation at the center of evolutionary change, Darwinism threatened to relativize variation; any idiosyncratic organic characteristic *might* be selected for. As Darwinian thought was absorbed into the productivist complex of values bequeathed by the Enlightenment, the imposition of developmentalism led to the stigmatization of many variations as "degenerations." Conversely, as the productivist ideology itself has receded, really only in this century, the more radical side of Darwin's thought has come to the fore and what was earlier seen as degeneration has come by degrees to be viewed as variation.

The history of sexology and related disciplines in the last quarter of the nineteenth century furnishes abundant evi-

18. Ellis and Symonds, *Sexual Inversion*, p. 136.

dence that the distinction between degeneration and variation was a fuzzy one. These disciplines depended on the central evolutionary assumption that "ontogeny recapitulates phylogeny" to fuel their concept of degeneration. That assumption was of course a highly developmentalist interpretation of Darwin's thought and very teleological. From this perspective, though, "failure" to recapitulate the last "acquisitions" of phylogeny could explain degeneration. There were two variations on this theme, one emphasizing the *atavistic* and the other the *dissolute* character of the degenerate. The first view was upheld by the famed criminologist and part-time sexologist Cesare Lombroso (1835–1910). Lombroso attempted to construct an evolutionary criminology, under which was subsumed the study of sexual deviations, by linking crime to atavism. According to him, the "born criminal shows . . . numerous specific characteristics that are almost always atavistic." Moreover, "many of the characteristics presented by savage races are very often found among born criminals." Crime—and sex deviation—were thus to be understood as reversion to an earlier ancestral pattern.[19]

A somewhat different view of degeneration was put forth by the American neurologist J. Hughlings Jackson (1835–1911), who suggested that the last "acquisition," that is, the most recently acquired and highly organized mental structure possessed by the species, normally organizes the elements of the submerged, earlier-acquired structures. Thus, Jackson believed, disruption of the highly organized structure of the "last acquisition" exposes the earlier structures which, superimposed on one another, are without any organizing principle. A failure to recapitulate fully the last stages of evolution would therefore create not a primitive personality but a dissolved nonpersonality.[20]

19. Cesare Lombroso, *Crime: Its Causes and Remedies* (Montclair, N.J.: Patterson Smith, 1968; rpt. of 1911 ed.), pp. 365–66.
20. J. Hughlings Jackson, *Neurological Fragments* (London: Oxford University Press, 1925), pp. 10–11, 140–45. Michel Foucault, *Mental Illness and*

Sexology fluctuated between the atavism and the dissolution theories in its stigmatization of sexual variations. On the one hand, these variations appeared to be regressions to earlier phases of evolution. Accordingly, sadism might be analyzed as an atavistic reappearance of the fused hunger and sexual instincts, while coprophilia might appear as reversion to the fused excretory and genital zones in certain lower organisms. On the other hand, sexual variations were sometimes stigmatized as a "dissolution of heredity" rather than "a form of heredity," that is, as disintegration of personality rather than a return to an older form of personality.[21]

Actually, a case can be made that psychoanalysis preserves both forms of degeneration, if only under assumed names. These theories of degeneration play a role in that science by describing phases of regression. Regression to earlier forms of object-love, associated in classical psychoanalysis with curable or at least analyzable neuroses, bears some resemblance to an atavistic regression to a primitive personality; in contrast, severe regression to the autoerotic phase before the construction of the personality, a condition associated with schizophrenia, bears some similarity to the dissolution of personality described by Jackson and others.[22]

III

By simultaneously discovering both the primacy and the primitiveness of the consumer, sexology revealed its contradictory structure and its ambivalence. Discovering dedifferentiated desire as the basis for existence, sexologists stigma-

Psychology, trans. Alan Sheridan (New York: Harper & Row, 1976), pp. 24–25, addresses this topic usefully. Sulloway, *Freud*, is also useful.

21. For a summary, see Sulloway, *Freud*, pp. 290–98; see also Krafft-Ebing, *Psychopathia Sexualis*, pp. 54–55, 226–27; Kiernan, "Psychological Aspects," p. 218.

22. See Foucault, *Mental Illness*.

tized that desire as degenerate. Accordingly, they sang a hymn to progress, but they sang uneasily. Their hymn to differentiation was undercut by the very nature of the concept of desire they embraced. Pre-Darwinian concepts of desire had stressed *difference*. Brotherly love could not be reduced to sexual love any more than male could be confused with female. But, as I noted above, the real contribution of Darwin, for good or ill, was his extension of individualism, similarity, and interchangeability to embrace the realm of desire. Darwin destroyed *difference* in the realm of desire, leaving differentiation as a kind of compensation. Indeed, the doctrine of sexual *differentiation* functioned as a kind of cultural bandage, preserving a pale reflection of difference into the twentieth century. But the history of sexology is in fact the history of how this concept of differentiation itself eroded. After all, the primacy of desire, of consumption, of discharge was underscored by the sexological conception of the very first pleasure and all succeeding pleasures as disaccumulation. This in turn gave a common unity to all desire and undercut distinctions between desires.

Only the doctrine of a progressive differentiation of desires and the sexes could prevent the dissolution of distinctions. But this doctrine was itself dependent upon the survival of a pre-Dawinian remnant of Lamarckianism informed by an Enlightenment vision of progress. The whole doctrine of sexual differentiation depended upon a developmentalism that was itself fading in the latter part of the nineteenth century. The very nature of the consumerist complex of values was hostile to this developmentalism and tended to erode it. Consider this idea of desire as discharge. The stress on disaccumulation as the end of all nervous energy makes it difficult to see the progress from less to more complexity as a law of nature. Yet Freud himself never fully abandoned developmentalism. On the contrary, his science remained suspended between developmentalism and its negation precisely because the whole point of his enterprise was to resist cultural entropy in the domain of desire by organizing that domain. Despite his need for the idea of progress, Freud was part of the intellectual climate that was undercutting that idea. To fin-de-siècle and early twentieth-century intellectuals across disciplinary lines and national boundaries in North America and Western Europe, the history of the world appeared to be moving in a parabolic course. Up to their time there had been progress; now that progress seemed to be threatened. In particular, the sexologists recognized the emergence of a plethora of new tendencies that seemed to reverse the cultural movement from less complex to more complex. More and more, they discovered variations that they could only stigmatize as degenerations.[23]

Charles Féré's doctrine of "diminishing reproduction" tells the whole story. According to this somber doctrine, the more advanced cultures must eliminate themselves; it was inevitable. "Civilisation acts upon the reproduction function," Féré argued, "by multiplying its variations and diminishing its fecundity." In short, "the more rapidly civilisation [evolution?] develops, the greater the degeneration." Thus, the highest civilizations must pass away to make room for others much as the Marshallian firm develops and then degenerates, making room for other firms. In a universe of scarcity, the universe discovered by intellectuals in the late nineteenth century, growth must always be followed by degeneration. This vision of scarcity, shaped perhaps by a sense of the poignancy of desire, is one in which civilization and the whole evolutionary process are subjected to a universal law of diminishing returns.[24] In 1895, H. G. Wells summed up the new pessimism in *The Time Machine*, describing how the protagonist "thought but cheerlessly of the Advancement of Mankind, and saw in the growing pile

23. See Traian Stoianovich, *French Historical Method: The Annales Paradigm* (Ithaca: Cornell University Press, 1976), p. 33.
24. Féré, *Sexual Instinct*, pp. 60–61.

of civilization only a foolish heaping that must inevitably fall back and destroy its makers in the end." It was perhaps precisely because Wells really understood the implications of Darwin's work that *The Time Machine* represents such a stark repudiation of the Enlightenment vision of development.[25]

IV

In spite of their ambivalance, sexologists could not escape the necessity of resisting the dissolution of the Enlightenment conceptions of need, gender, and development in the domain of sex. Accentuating the conservative aspect of their thought, the scientists of sex attempted to reduce all sex variations to degrees of degeneration; a threefold distinction between atypical, atavistic and morbid degeneration appears to have been widespread. In this scheme, the first category was apparently associated with variations in general, the second with the reappearance of primitive characteristics in an individual, and the third with the breakdown of the individual. By separating atavistic from morbid or "dissolute" conditions, Féré was also able to separate the primitive from the criminal. In contrast, Ellis confused these categories in his discussion of criminality as late as 1897. On the other hand, he tended to distinguish mere variation and true (atavistic-morbid) degeneration, regarding some perversion as variation, and criminality and mental illness as degeneration. Within the sphere of sexology proper, there was a long-term tendency to distinguish further among perversions as to the degree of degeneration, the tendency being to treat the least severe "degenerations" as variations. In other words, the ideological defense against sexual democratization was slowly democratized.[26]

25. H. G. Wells, *Three Prophetic Science Fiction Novels* (New York: Dover, 1960), p. 335.

26. Féré, *Sexual Instinct*, pp. 39–42, 286–87; Ellis, *Criminal*, pp. 35, 52, 252–53; Ellis and Symonds, *Sexual Inversion*, pp. 133–37; Lombroso, *Crime*, pp. 370–71.

In the course of the twentieth century, structuralist anthropology has taken up and developed the relativism implicit in Darwinian thought. Just as Darwin really meant that each species can be judged only in relation to its environment, so modern anthropology has increasingly argued that each culture can be judged only in terms of its success or failure in meeting its environmental challenges. As Darwinism implicitly destroyed the Enlightenment hierarchy of development linking different species, so twentieth-century anthropology destroys the scheme of development connecting different cultures. The domination of development-in-time over spatially separate cultures and organisms is thus shattered, permiting a radical relativization of value.

In this sense, structuralism represents a more unambiguous affirmation and a wider extension of democratic values than does sexology. It is thus not surprising that in stark contrast to anthropology, psychology continues to make use of developmentalist and thus normative models. But between the "primitive" and the child, the position of the pervert and thus the polymorphous tastes of the consumer continue to remain ambiguous. Sexologists have thus tended to polarize, in the United States at least, between those under the influence of Alfred Kinsey, who have emphasized a more relativistic approach, and those under the influence of Freud, who have upheld a more normative-developmentalist scheme. Even though no real synthesis has yet emerged, the center of gravity has clearly shifted toward the more relativistic orientation, an orientation that better reflects the "existential" or subjective value theory of the consumer.[27]

27. For the revolt against the idea of progress and development-in-time, see Claude Lévi-Strauss, *Race et histoire* (Paris: Gonthier, 1961).

CHAPTER FOUR

Democratization
and Degeneration

In this chapter, I shall reassemble the separate intellectual elements—the dissolutions of gender, species need, and development-in-time—which played a role in the transition from a productivist to a consumerist culture in order to show how these elements converged to create a highly contradictory conception of the family in late-nineteenth-century sexology.[1] A central thesis of this book is that Enlightenment intellectuals generally understood the family in holistic terms. Arguing that society was a competitive domain inhabited by possessive individuals, intellectuals from Hobbes to Marx assumed that the family was a cooperative realm. Its cooperative nature arose from the functional differences among its several members, differences that already existed in the so-called state of nature. As late as the mid-nineteenth century, no one denied that there was a fundamental (i.e., natural) distinction between men and women on the one hand and parents and children on the other. If society (economy) arose from a contract between

---

1. I should, at the outset, emphasize that this chapter deals with the *conception* of the family in sexology, and not with the actual structure or constitution of the different types of family which prevailed in late-nineteenth-century Western Europe. For this, see Edward Shorter, *Making of the Modern Family* (New York: Basic, 1975).

individuals, each of whom embodied all of society and who were thus equal to one another, the family had arisen with humanity itself because men and women, parents and children, could not have existed without one another, even from the beginning. Even Rousseau, who denied the transhistorical character of the family itself, did not deny that men and women existed in the state of nature. On the contrary, it was the assumption of a natural and eternal *difference* between the two sexes that provided Rousseau with the justification for excluding the female sex from the realm of citizenship. Classical thought could go no further.[2]

But the publication and diffusion of Darwinian conceptions about humanity's transsexual ancestry marked a break with earlier conceptions of gender. Armed with Darwinian theory, one could believe that the individual recapitulated all earlier modes of reproduction: the primitive fission mode in which self-preservation and self-reproduction were fused; the conjugation mode, which appeared, Albert Moll wrote, to be either "an act of nutrition or assimilation . . . or . . . in a category with the impregnation of the egg cell with the

2. Classical thought has given us historical accounts of humanity's movement from a primitive nature to a civilized society. What do these accounts signify about the culture of the West? I suggest that these accounts have symbolically depicted contradictory conceptions of the social order, the newer (more radical) conceptions of that order having been stigmatized as primitive, the older (more conservative) conceptions being upheld as civilized. In classical thought during the seventeenth and eighteenth centuries, the state of nature was thus usually associated with an equality within the masculine sphere, an equality that was then restricted or "taken away" by the more limited conception of citizenship associated with civilized society. But even in the state of nature citizenship was masculine, the limits imposed by gender being considered natural by classical thinkers. It was impossible to envision a fundamentally genderless human nature and thus a basis for universal citizenship until the emergence of a Darwinian thought that revealed humankind's transsexual ancestry in the state of nature. Hence the revision of the categories after 1859–71, genderlessness (previously inconceivable) now being stigmatized as primitive, while universal equality among males (previously understood as primitive) was now recognized as comparatively civilized. For several essays on the classical conception of gender, see Clark and Lange, *Sexism*, pp. 16–116, especially "Rousseau: Women and the General Will," pp. 41–52.

sperm cell, as in higher animals"; and the sexual mode, originally hermaphroditic, when desire for the other was superimposed on the autoerotic aims of self-satisfaction and self-reproduction. It was now possible to discover the original and fundamental genderlessness of human nature. The Darwinian state of nature was in fact populated by transsexual consumers, a condition that undercut the justification for excluding women and children from the realm of citizenship.[3]

The publication of the *Origin of Species* in 1859 and the *Descent of Man, and Selection in Relation to Sex* in 1871 marked the emergence of a universal conception of individuality based on a radically new understanding of human nature. But this new human nature appeared frighteningly alien and inhuman to its fin-de-siècle discoverers. More specifically, the new genderless human nature was apparently incompatible with the holistic ideal of the family bequeathed from the Enlightenment. By implying that every individual embodied both sexes, the new individualism threatened (and still threatens) to transform the family into just one more realm of contract between fundamentally similar, idiosyncratic, neuter human beings.

We have already seen, however, that this was only one side of the story. Taken as a whole, sexology was highly ambivalent toward the family because it attempted to bring order to the very realm it was democratizing. In other words, sexlogy was a force for cultural conservation, its conservative character functioning as a kind of cultural bandage over the break with the bourgeois past. Accordingly, sexology imposed on the genderless human beings it discovered a law of development, reintroducing the hierarchy of development-in-time in its last and most desperate incarnation as a defense against the tendency toward universal democratization implicit in the new concept of the individual. In opposition to the leveling tendencies of Darwinism, the

---

3. Moll, *Libido Sexualis*, p. 60.

principles of developmental evolution postulated inferior hierarchical positions for proletarians, perverts, women, children, criminals, primitives, and the mentally ill which justified their exclusion from society anew. To be sure, this exclusion was ostensibly no longer based on *difference*, but on a progressive *differentiation* from a common sameness.

To put it a different way, sexology attempted to reconstruct reproduction from the point of view of consumption and thus the family from the perspective of the idiosyncratic consumer. But what form of reproduction and what sort of family? That of property owners. Sexual science fixed an abstract representation of the middle-class family as the eternal standard for all cultures and peoples. Accordingly, sexologists in general would hold the limit of democracy to the masculine society of the propertied even as they extended that society to the furthest limits by implicitly including women and children. It was in this context that not only the norms of middle-class Western culture but those of a particular phase in the history of that culture, a phase associated with the remarkable sexual dimorphism that developed in transatlantic propertied circles after 1750, became the universal standard of masculinity and femininity. Here were the landmarks of the erotic universe. And it was precisely because these landmarks were alredy being covered over that sexology was called upon to uncover them and polish them up.

In efforts to prevent the erosion of the separate sexes, the sexologists could draw from a long tradition. I have noted above how social thought during the period from the seventeenth to the nineteenth century took for granted a gendered perspective. Even the international order was divided into masculine and feminine civilizations, the former in the north and the west, the latter in the south and the east. As early as the mid-eighteenth century Edward Gibbon contrasted the "effeminine" East with the "martial" West, and during the French Revolution polemicist Barnave wrote of the people in the Orient whose "physical disposition . . . is an obstacle to both the power of wealth and to that energy of character by which a people succeed in tempering despotism with democracy." For Hegel, "the History of the World travels from East to West; for Europe is absolutely the end of History, Asia the beginning." In the eighteenth century, Western intellectuals apparently distinguished between the "despotisms" of Asia where, as Hegel put it, only "One is free" and the "monarchies" of Europe where "All are free." But in the West, "all" referred only to all members of the masculine sphere of production. Thus, for Hegel, "the family" was "excluded from that process of development in which History takes its rise." Beyond this, Hegel believed, "even if an equal share in the government is accorded all citizens, women and children are immediately passed by, and remain excluded." By the nineteenth century, then, Western ideologies apparently tended to conceive of freedom as a kind of secondary male characteristic, consequently associating masculinity with the activity of citizenship and femininity with the passivity of biological males in a despotism. It was in this context that sexology simultaneously furthered and resisted the extension of the concept of citizenship beyond the masculine sphere to include women and children.[4]

Of course, a new idea is often distorted by related ideas it inherits; as Robert Holt has noted, in this way newer conceptions are constantly reabsorbed into "the stock of already existing concepts, so that a revolutionary proposal may end up reinforcing a reactionary idea." At the same time, the "revolutionary proposal" also alters the "stock of already existing concepts" so that intellectual shifts are

---

4. Edward Gibbon, *Decline and Fall of the Roman Empire* (New York: Random House, Modern Library Edition), pp. 521–22; Emmanuel Chill, ed., *Power, Property and History: Barnave's 'Introduction to the French Revolution' and Other Writings* (New York: Harper & Row, 1971), p. 84; Hegel, *Philosophy of History*, pp. 59, 103–4, 145; Philip Greven, *The Protestant Temperament: Patterns of Child-rearing, Religious Experience, and the Self in Early America* (New York: New American Library, 1977), pp. 336, 351.

possible. Something like this probably happened in sexology. At first, it drew much of its inspiration from the gendered perspective inherited from the previous epoch. For instance, in the sexual-anthropological literature of the last quarter of the nineteenth century, the theme of gender was often linked to climate. It is in this curious context, itself a kind of intellectual remnant of the Enlightenment, that we should situate Sir Richard Burton's famous and curious "Terminal Essay." In that work, Burton hypothesized the existence of a "Sotadic Zone" in which what he called pederasty was "popular and endemic" as well as "geographical and climatic." Although the zone was identified with warm climate and centered around the Mediterranean and tropical regions, most of the Orient and Pre-Columbian America was also included in it. In other words, the Sotadic Zone took in most of the cultures outside the West. Burton mused that within that zone "there is a blending of the masculine and the feminine temperments, a crasis which occurs elsewhere only sporadically." Similar ideas shaped the thinking of sexologists such as Paolo Mantegazza and Iwan Bloch who were interested in cross-cultural studies of sexuality.[5]

Against this background, turn-of-the-century sexologists including Ellis, Krafft-Ebing, and Freud were dedicated to in effect absorbing evolutionary theory and its implicit conception of genderless humanity into the ideology of sexual dimorphism inherited from the Enlightenment. Thus, in general, sexual science advanced a conceptualization of the evolution of sex in which the sexual differentiation of the middle-class family was taken as the culmination of a natural process that had begun with the first self-reproducing amoeba. The "virilization" of the West, associated

5. Robert Holt, *Abstracts of the Complete Psychological Works of Sigmund Freud* (New York: Jason Aronson, 1973), p. 23; Darwin, *Descent of Man*, p. 167; Sir Richard Burton, *The Book of a Thousand Nights and a Night*, 10 vols. (Benares, 1885), 10:205–10; Iwan Bloch, *Anthropological Studies in the Strange Sexual Practices of All Races and All Ages*, trans. Keene Wallis (New York: Anthropological Press, 1933), p. 27.

with the emergence of several middle-class ideologies during the period 1750–1850, was thus taken as an eternal and natural process. Darwin himself had already formulated the concept of sexual selection in order to explain how sexual reproduction must inevitably further sexual differentiation. Against the background of this highly teleological conception of differentation, sexologists tended to agree with Krafft-Ebing's blanket assertion that "the differentiation of the sexes and the development of sexual types is evidently the result of an infinite successsion of intermediary stages of evolution."[6] For Krafft-Ebing and his epigones, civilization appeared as nothing more than the continuation of this process of differentiation. Like Darwin, sexologists united the doctrine of gender to the ideology of progress, so that progress was interpreted as the movement from genderlessness to gender. Conversely, "primitive" cultures were associated with a lack of sexual distinctions. In those cultures, it was widely believed, there was a certain similarity between the sexes. Havelock Ellis, for example, noted that "among some races of India, the Pueblos of North America, the Patagonians, the women are as large as the men." Even in Europe, Ellis wrote, "among the Russians the sexes are more alike than among the English or the French." One of the most interesting students of "primitive love," the American Henry Finck, concluded around the turn of the century that "the lower the race is the more do its individuals thus resemble one another. Nay, this approximation goes so far as to make even the two sexes much less distinct." Thus a lack of differentiation was associated with the primitive, and the movement toward civilization and middle-class society was linked to the growing differentiation of the two sexes. But implicit in this hypothesis was a contradiction. With the progress of sexual differentiation, women must become more feminine, but with the progress of individuation, they must become more active. Finck's concept of romantic love

6. Krafft-Ebing, *Psychopathia Sexualis*, p. 28.

as involving both free choice and fully differentiated sexes is based upon two irreconcilable elements, it demands that women be simultaneously more active and more passive.[7]

I

We have seen how sexology attempted to construct an ideology of sexual differentiation as a substitute for and continuation of the older ideology of sexual difference. It remains to focus on how the new ideology of sexual differentiation could be used to control and organize the sexual realm in the latter part of the nineteenth century. I shall argue that sexology perceived the coming disintegration of the middle-class sexual order and sought to stigmatize that disintegration. For example, in *Man and Woman*, Havelock Ellis argued that: "As . . . social changes tend more and more to abolish artificial sexual differences, thus acting inversely to the well-marked tendency observed in passing from the lower to the higher races, we are brought face to face with the consideration of those differences which are not artificial, and which no equalization of social conditions can entirely remove, the natural characters and predispositions which will always inevitably influence the sexual allotment of human activities." Ellis clearly recognized two tendencies, a "well-marked tendency" toward sexual differentiation, and, "acting inversely," a newer tendency toward sexual democratization. The first trend must be associated with the ideological and to a lesser extent cultural differentiation of masculine and feminine spheres of action among the Western middle classes in the period from, say, 1750 to 1880, the second trend with the erosion of the separate

7. Havelock Ellis, *Man and Woman* (New York: Arno, 1974; rpt. of 4th ed., 1904), pp. 4–5; Henry Finck, *Primitive Love and Love Stories* (New York: Scribner, 1899), pp. 59, 65–67, 119, 132–33, 335, 345.

spheres during the last decades of the nineteenth century. Now, it was Ellis's intention to strip away the "artificial" *difference* between the sexes, but only to reveal the reality of sexual *differentiation* founded on the evolutionary process itself. Ellis thus implied that the "inverse trend," taken too far, would be unnatural.[8] Others agreed that the emergence of a genderless social order associated with the integration of women and children into the masculine sphere of citizenship could only represent a dedifferentiation of the sexual realm and a consequent reversion to the primitive. Accordingly, James Kiernan expressed the sentiment that the "ideal of the female 'reformers'" should be associated with "an atavistic reversion to conditions beneath birds and mammals."[9]

In his monumental study, *Primitive Love and Love Stories*, Henry Finck expressed similar sentiments, affirming in a marvelous passage: "Nature has been at work on this problem of differentiating the sexes ever since it created the lowest animal organisms, and this fact, which stands as firm as a rock, gives us the consoling assurance that the present abnormal attempts to make women masculine by giving them the same education, employments, sports, ideals and political aspirations as men have, must end in ignominious failure. If the viragoes had their way, men and women would in the course of time revert to the conditions of the lowest savages, differing only in their organs of generation." Interesting enough as an example of "scientific" polemic, this passage also makes fascinatingly clear how late-nineteenth-century writers on the sexes imposed on Darwinism a rigorously teleological scheme of developmentalism which assumed that the middle-class family and sexual order was latent even in the "lowest animal organisms." Indeed, normative sexology depended on this developmentalist scheme, because the various sexes and tastes had to be arranged in a

8. Ellis, *Man and Woman*, pp. 17–18.
9. Kiernan, "Psychological Aspects," p. 193.

temporal and thus a moral order based on their degree of differentiation.[10]

Iwan Bloch went even further than Finck, arguing that "a quite serious etiological factor in the genesis of triabidism [female homosexuality] is the modern feminist movement." Charles Féré agreed that the "feminist movement . . . is at once a symptom of and a factor in the dissolution of sex. It represents the tendency to the levelling of the sexes." Clearly, there was a more or less general tendency among sexologists to identify democratization with degeneration.[11]

It was in this context that Colin Scott proposed that recent cultural evolution had imposed on the "primary law of courting," in which men were active-anaclitic and women passive-narcissistic, a " secondary law of courting." According to Scott, the new tendency "is sometimes expressed by saying that men are becoming more like women, women more like men." In an advanced civilization, Scott argued, the "female develops a superadded activity, the male becoming relatively passive and imaginatively attentive to the psychical and bodily states of the female." Though Scott was tolerant of these changes, other sexologists took them as symptomatic of the degeneration that multiplies as civilization advances.[12] Certainly, degeneration was associated with an "inverse tendency" toward dedifferentiation.

II

The widespread doctrine of sexual differentiation was necessary as a means of reinstituting or, better, conserving the hierarchy of sexual difference. But to perform this function, the doctrine of differentiation had to be constructed in a particular way; it was necessary that the differ-

---

10. Finck, *Primitive Love*, p. 66.
11. Bloch, *Anthropological Studies*, p. 240; Féré, *Sexual Instinct*, p. 52.
12. Scott, "Sex and Art," pp. 207–8.

entiation of the sexes be *asymmetrical.* According to the prevailing conception, which first appeared in the work of Darwin himself, the male was more differentiated and thus more advanced than the female. Against this background, sexology linked women to children and primitives, regarding the feminine as less removed than the masculine from the originally hermaphroditic ancestry of humankind. Thus, evolutionary theory was assimilated to the Enlightenment complex of ideas which contrasted an evolving masculine sphere of history with a static feminine sphere of family.[13]

The doctrine of asymmetrical differentiation provided the tools with which sexual science was able to draw an analogy between the woman, the child, and the primitive. Like the primitive and the child, woman appeared less mature (differentiated). For example, sexologists generally perceived female desire as more diffuse and consequently weaker than male desire. They also took the "survival" of periodicity in the woman as evidence of her primitive nature, seeing the period as a remnant of the animal past without analogy in the male.[14] The "narcissistic" character of women linked them to earlier epochs. This narcissism in particular made women appear childlike. For the sexologists, the multiplicity of female erogenous zones suggested that women were less differentiated and thus closer to the amoeba. It was in this context, indeed, that the clitoris took on a particularly important significance as a remnant of androgyny without analogy in the more differentiated male. Because the clitoris was linked to the ancestral hermaphrodite, it was something the truly "feminine," and thus truly differentiated, woman was expected to "overcome." Bloch, for example, argued that the clitoris of female apes was larger than that of

13. Darwin, *Descent of Man*, vol. I, pp. 271–73.

14. None the less, male periodicity was not completely ignored; thus see the work of Wilhelm Fliess, Freud's friend, especially as it is discussed in Freud, *Origins of Psychoanalysis*, pp. 6–8, 14, 35–38, 40–43, 45, 120, 158–60, 179–80, 190, 210, 229–30.

women, implying that evolution was progressively eliminating the organ. Psychoanalysis merely followed in this tradition when it assumed that truly mature (feminine) women must "overcome" their phallic or clitoral sexuality to reach complete differentiation.[15]

An understanding of this conception of female sexuality should also shed light on the work of Havelock Ellis, who is often characterized as a kind of feminist because he apparently emphasized the sexual endowment of women.[16] Actually, Ellis fits rather neatly into the general pattern of sexology delineated above. Sexologists, including Ellis, tended to attribute to women, as well as to children and primitives, a more extensive though less intense sexuality than that possessed by men. Actually, it is probably more accurate to say more extensive and *thus* less intensive because sexual energy was supposed to obey the laws of an "ecology of desire." In this ecological conception, outlined above, the value of stored charge and thus potential discharge is effectively diminished if it is either insufficiently concentrated or insufficently delayed. Ellis's conception of female sexuality as diffuse and tending toward narcissism, autoeroticism, and perversion was consistent with the widely held emphasis on female passivity as weakness. Ellis himself noted that "a slight degree of homosexuality is commoner in women than in men" even though "fully developed cases of inversion are rarer in women than in men," a fact he attributed to "the greater plasticity of the feminine organism to slight stimuli, and its lesser liability to serious variations." Such a dichotomization, of course, was perfectly consistent with the generally held view that males

15. For Krafft-Ebing on the female erogenous zones, see *Psychopathia Sexualis*, pp. 24–26; for a discussion of the greater sensitivity of women, see Ellis, *Man and Woman*, 4th ed., pp. 269, 310, 6th ed., pp. 398, 399–425; Scott, "Sex and Art," pp. 204–6; Stephen Gould, *The Mismeasure of Man* (New York: Norton, 1981), p. 118.

16. See especially Robinson, *Modernization of Sex*, pp. 1–41.

evolved further because they were in fact more sensitive than females to "serious variations."[17]

Now these theories all tended to presuppose a female evolutionary conservatism in contrast to a male evolutionary dynamism. Yet this dynamism implied degeneration as well as generation, devolution as well as evolution. Accordingly, late-nineteenth-century students of Darwin sometimes identified genius with degeneration. In his work on female criminals, Lombroso concluded that if criminality was an atavism, it had to be less common among women for the same reason that genius was less common among them; women were more primitive precisely because they were less likely to vary greatly in their characteristics.[18]

For Lombroso, the characteristics of the criminal woman are those of the primitive woman. The criminal woman, in so far as she existed, Lombroso believed, appeared more masculine than her sisters, an atavistic incarnation of her savage semi-differentiated ancestors. Still, the worst forms of criminality, like the best forms of genius, rarely appeared in women. To some extent, though, variations among women might be limited by the social environment. Lombroso admitted that women were constrained by the limits of their femininity, so that the "primitive woman was rarely a murderess; but she was always a prostitute." For Lombroso, in fact, prostitution was the feminine equivalent of masculine crime: the prostitute expressed the atavistic reversion to an androgynous sexuality in a world that would not accept other forms of feminine aggressiveness.[19]

17. Havelock Ellis, "Sexual Inversion in Women," *Alienist and Neurologist* 16 (1895), 142–43.

18. Cesare Lombroso and William Ferrero, *The Female Offender* (New York: Philosophical Library, 1958), pp. 108–13, 186–87.

19. In modern times, Lombroso believed, "prostitution largely takes the place of crime for women." Thus, the relationship between crime and prostitution in women that Lombroso delineated was not unlike the Freudian relation between perversion and neurosis. Here were the germs of an interesting theory of crime prevention, based on the idea that criminal tendencies might be directed toward socially useful goals: the criminal sadist might be channeled into the socially useful skill of surgery, etc. For

III

Just as evolutionary theorists and sexologists had an ambivalent attitude toward the homogenization of the sexes, so they had an ambivalent attitude toward the homogenization of the generations.[20] On the one hand, late-nineteenth-century psychologists stressed that the child still lived in the adult; on the other hand it stressed the primitiveness of the child. The history of the species, evolutionary theorists argued, was a history of gradual differentiation. Accordingly, dedifferentiation implied degeneration. It was within this framework that childishness, perversion, and crime could be linked. There was apparently a general consensus that children were less differentiated than adults and, thus, correspondingly more primitive. Of course, for some this primitiveness was unredeemably evil while for others it had a sort of charm. On the one hand Lombroso painted a particularly gloomy picture, portraying the child as inherently criminal; on the other hand the great American authority on adolescence, G. Stanley Hall, was content to picture children as rather lively savages.[21]

Within the parameters allowed by theory, the libidinal "ecology" of primitives, perverts, and, by analogy, children, appeared to be similar. Childish or primitive desires were characterized by their immediacy, as well as by their diffuse and plastic character. The "impulsiveness" of these desires

Lombroso, then, prostitution and criminality were alternative expressions of the same primitive constitution in certain women. See in particular Lombroso and Ferrero, ibid., pp. 108–13; Lombroso, *Crime*, pp. 191–92, 368–69, 448.

20. Bourgeois culture may have been particularly characterized by a dichotomization between adult males on the one side and women and children on the other. See in particular, Nicholson, *Gender and History*, passim.

21. Lombroso, *Crime*, pp. 368–69; G. Stanley Hall, *Adolescence: Its Psychology and Its Relations to Physiology, Anthropology, Sociology, Sex, Crime and Religion and Education*, 2 vols. (New York: D. Appleton, 1905), 1:334–51; see also Ellis, *Criminal*, p. 258.

reduced their potency because the primitive constitution could not wait long enough to accumulate the charge necessary for a potent and focused discharge, just as it could not wait long enough to accumulate capital. But the very impulsiveness that was attributed to primitiveness was also an argument for the primacy of consumption as the original *human* characteristic. Saturated with these contradictory convictions, sexology came to stigmatize as childish and primitive the very consumerist values it represented.

No belief better illustrates the paradoxical position of children as well as women in late-nineteenth-century sexology and psychology than the widespread idea of "precocity." In this idea we see the real shallowness of evolutionary optimism in an increasingly somber intellectual climate. In his article "Precocity and Prematuration," the American psychologist Lewis Terman explored these concepts. "The possibility of precocity," Terman wrote in 1905, "presupposes the existence of a period of immaturity and incompleteness." For Terman, "the amoeba, which begins its independent life as a perfect individual, is never subject to prematurity."[22] The period of immaturity is extended as we ascend the evolutionary ladder from the less to the more intelligent and complex organisms on the "animal scale." Consequently, the "lower" animals, sexes, and even, or perhaps especially, races, matured earlier. Terman thus took note of "the rapid school progress made by the negro child for the first few years, in many cases even outdoing his white competitors." Eventually, however, "the tide turns and the negro child relapses into a state of chronic stupidity, while the white child pushes on to heights the former will never see."[23]

Armed with this smug ideology, Terman affirmed that

22. Lewis Terman, "A Study in Precocity and Prematuration," *American Journal of Psychology* 16 (April 1905), 148.

23. Ibid., p. 151. See also Bloch, *Anthropological Studies*, pp. 26–27; Ellis, *Man and Woman*, 1st ed., p. 177, quoted in Terman, "A Study in Precocity," p. 151; Ellis, *Man and Woman*, 6th ed., p. 238.

forced maturation placed too much of a neurophysiological burden on the nervous system and could lead only to disaster in the form of nervous exhaustion. Less developed peoples, he reasoned, will be ruined if they are exposed to the culture of a developed civilization. Chronic fatigue brought on by over-education might lead to juvenile delinquency, and chronic overstimulation could bring on perversity. Such views, solidly rooted in the prevailing distortion of evolutionary theory, were common enough. A generation earlier, Kiernan had argued that the "normal psychological condition of the negro was one resembling that of many Aryan and Shemetic insane." From Kiernan's perspective—one which, by the way, carelessly confused atavism, dissolution, and variation—there was an "undeniable increase of crime, pauperism and insanity among negroes *since* the [Civil] war." Kiernan was apparently of a mind that exposure to white culture, or freedom, was too much for the former slaves. He was not the only one. Even those sexologists less tainted by the prevailing American obsession with race found the precocity doctrine useful. And, it was of course commonly held that women, like primitives, started out ahead, only to fall behind civilized men.[24]

In the end, the doctrine of precocity was one more technique used by the sexologists and their intellectual allies to preserve a remnant of holism in an increasingly democratized culture. As I noted above, individualism implies both the liberty to become anything within the social order and the social equality of common ancestry. Individualism does not necessitate competition, but competition certainly depends upon individualism as it has been defined in this book; in a sense, we recognize as free and equal those with whom we compete. Conversely, the doctrine of precocity paid a false compliment to women, children, and those races designated as inferior by denying their ability to

24. James Kiernan, "Race and Insanity," *Journal of Nervous and Mental Diseases* 12 (1885), 174–75.

compete with other citizens and thus to take part in the social universe. A particularly seductive doctrine, this hypothesis of precocity, since it argued that women, children, and "primitives" could be protected only if their inferiority were recognized and could be free only by submitting. And what a clever argument for the separate education or de-education of women, children, and others whom the middle-class world of the sexologists would exclude from the realm of citizenship.[25]

I have called the idea of precocity a remnant of holism because it used—or distorted—the doctrine of differentiation in order to make it function as a substitute for the older doctrine of difference. But this idea of differentiation from a common sameness was a two-edged sword. Evolutionary theory posed a dilemma for the sexologists and their colleagues in the related fields of psychology and criminology. On the one hand, to relate all forms of desire (as well as all species, sexes, and races) to each other was to give them a generic unity that subverted difference; on the other hand, it was now possible to control these desires (and the species, sexes, and races they represented) by relating them to each other in the developmentalist hierarchy. Here was the key to the "sexualization" of women and children at the end of the nineteenth century. In sexology, women and children became sexualized even as they continued as sexless denizens of the innocent world outside competitive society. Sexuality was simultaneously universal and the function of the adult male alone. The problem was the necessity of upholding difference with a theory that emphasized differentiation from a common sameness. As long as the accent was on the differentiation, difference could be sustained; but there was a gradual tendency to shift the emphasis to the common sameness underlying the apparent difference.

25. See Illich, *Gender*, for a modern reformulation of this false compliment. In this recently published study, Illich argues that women must always come out second-rate when they directly compete with men. See also Gould, *Mismeasure*.

In sexology, this took the form of a movement from an adult male sexuality to a universally defined sexuality.

Trapped in the contradictions between these opposite conceptions, the sexologists blew hot and cold. Was there a "childhood sexuality"? Albert Moll, for one, was not exactly sure. "Before puberty," he admitted, ". . . it is often difficult to draw the line between sexual and social feelings." However, "even in extreme cases the love of the child for its mother may always be distinguished from the sexual love of a child for another." But Moll did not deny that "sometimes the line is very difficult to draw."[26]

The problem was that evolutionary thought was implicitly monist in a way that tended to deprive the idea "sexuality" of its original limited meaning. The phylogenetic origins of sexuality in primeval undifferentiated desire undercut any attempt to distinguish the sexual from the nonsexual. In this context, social energies might appear as nothing more than a rarified form of sexual energy. In other words, the social appeared as a higher stage of the sexual, arising out of but in opposition to primeval desire. In refusing to take these ideas to their logical conclusion, Moll paid a price in clarity and elegance, losing out in the course of the first decade of the twentieth century to the more ambitious synthesis of Sigmund Freud. Freud, unlike Moll, was willing to do on an explicit level what Darwinism had already done implicitly: that is, replace the idea of a difference between social and sexual desire with a concept in which social and sexual love become differentiated unequally from a common sameness. By replacing difference with differentiation Freud was able to explain precisely *how* relations within the family were connected to relations outside the family in a *hierarchical* order. What Freud called the Oedipus complex, however unpleasant an idea, was the best defense against an even more unbearable idea: the dissolution of the hierarchical order of the sexes.

26. Moll, *Libido Sexualis*, pp. 80–82.

By replacing the concept of sexual difference with that of sexual differentiation, sexology both resisted and furthered the extension of individualism to include individuals of both sexes *within* the family. In other words, without quite meaning to, the sexologists in general contributed to the reconceptualization of the family as a system of contractual relationships between the individuals within it. For example, sexual science often contrasted individual with so-called social impulses. Whereas classical thought understood the reproductive instinct as natural, outside of and prior to society, sexology treated the reproductive instinct as a social impulse, one recently and only with some difficulty acquired by the species. In contrast, the autoerotic or self-preservative instinct, which I have associated with consumption, appeared more natural and more truly instinctive than the social "instinct." This ideological shift reveals the revision of the conception of individualism after Darwin to include members *within* the family, which pre-Darwinian thought had excluded. Classical ideology had maintained that there could be only one citizen per household; post-Darwinian thought tended to see the household as a contract between individuals. In the process of the shift from a classical conception of individualism to a neoclassical form, reproduction lost its naturalness and became increasingly understood as a social or "artificial" synthesis of impulses. The reproductive instinct, the instinct to start a family, became increasingly problematical. That instinct appears, sexologists increasingly believed, only at the end of a long phylogenetic—and thus a long personal—evolution and only with the greatest of difficulty, because, as Freud said, "every step on this long path of development can be an occasion for a dissociation of the sexual instinct."[27] Accordingly, the social sphere expanded to include the inner determination of the family, leaving outside society only the inner determination of the now genderless consumer.

Against this background, sexology appears to have under-

27. Freud, *Three Essays*, p. 101.

gone a gradual shift toward the separation of idiosyncratic desires from the ideology of familial need. This tendency was already evident in the work of Krafft-Ebing, who increasingly upheld the right of the individual to "sexual" happiness, thus defining that individual above all as a consumer.[28] The progress of this shift in values marked the gradual decline in the importance of the hereditary factor in sexology. Actually, the very appearance of sexology with its implicit conception of a genderless individuality marked the beginning of the end of the heredity concept. But around the turn of the century, there was a more explicit shift in emphasis from a phylogenetic or "racial" to an ontogenetic or "individual" conception of degeneration, which suggests that a further erosion of the importance of heredity was taking place. In the United States and Vienna, at least, this shift was associated with the increasing influence of psychoanalysis. Under these circumstances, the concept of racial degeneration receded before that of individual degeneration which, however well masked by the terms "fixation" and "regression," remained degeneration. It is not necessary here to make the argument that psychoanalysis retained some of the spirit of hereditary taint in its emphasis on the familial generation of neurosis, because it is enough to affirm that, by purging the increasingly outmoded emphasis on familial degeneration, Freud's system all the better preserved the idea of individual degeneration. Of course, the repudiation of the idea of familial degeneration represented a further step in the ideological disintegration of the family as a holistic system. But having made this retrenchment in their battle against the democratization of the family, psychoanalysts dug in their heels and held the line by identifying the further dissolution of the familial order with the dissolution of individual personalities within the family.[29]

28. Krafft-Ebing, *Psychopathia Sexualis*, pp. 383–88.
29. For another view of the relationship between psychoanalysis and degeneration theory, see Foucault, *History of Sexuality*, pp. 149–50. Sulloway, *Freud*, is also useful here, especially pp. 289–319.

CHAPTER FIVE

Sexuality and History

The last four chapters have been concerned mainly with what is fundamentally a structural analysis. In this chapter, I focus more precisely on a purely historical analysis of the emergence of sexual science. Recent scholarship, especially the work of Foucault and Jeffrey Weeks, suggests that in the course of the latter half of the nineteenth century and the beginning of the twentieth, an intellectual culture that distinguished between procreative and nonprocreative *acts* began to give way to one that distinguished between heterosexual and homosexual *preferences*. The emergence of the categories "heterosexual" and "homosexual" as what in effect were descriptions of consumer choices was characterized by the tendency of the homosexual to distinguish itself from run-of-the-mill perversions and to establish itself as an alternative to rather than an inferior form of heterosexual desire.[1]

The terms "heterosexual" and "homosexual" constituted

1. Compare Vern L. Bullough, "Homosexuality and the Medical Model," *Journal of Homosexuality* 1 (1974), 99–101; Bullough, *Homosexuality: A History* (New York: New American Library, 1979), pp. 1–16; Foucault, *History of Sexuality*, pp. 43, 101; Jeffrey Weeks, *Coming Out: Homosexual Politics in Britain, from the Nineteenth Century to the Present* (London: Quartet Books, 1977).

the elements of a classification scheme connecting the subject and the object of desire. Accordingly, they described preferences rather than acts. Appearing as early as 1869, the German *Homosexual* arrived in France as *homosexuel(le)* only by 1891 and in England only in 1897. *Heterosexual* had a similar history, appearing in German first, but not in English until 1892 and even later in French.[2] The tardy adoption of this terminology was by no means an accident. Taken literally, these terms would retire the idea of desire as a means to the ultimate end of procreation in favor of desire as an end in itself. But if the terms were evidence of an emerging consumerist ideology, they were put into service only to prevent the triumph of that ideology. The concept of "homosexual" and, in a more subtle way, that of "heterosexual" were simultaneously a step forward in the homogenization of the sexes and a cultural defense against still further sexual homogenization. Consequently, the categories of sexology, like the science itself, were highly contradictory.[3]

These contradictions would be better understood if we could develop a micro-periodization of the history of sexology which would help us trace the subtle redefinitions and reformulations of sexual science which appeared at the end of the nineteenth and the beginning of the twentieth century. Unfortunately, neither Foucault, Robinson, nor Weeks has worked out such a periodization in detail. Beginnings in this direction were made, however, in a recent article by George Chauncey. Chauncey suggests that if sexology functioned as a conservative defense against social change, it nevertheless altered the structure of its defenses "in a manner which reflected changes in the actual organization of sex/gender roles in society." Chauncey's work implies that the successive forms of sexual science may have reflected

2. Ellis and Symonds, *Sexual Inversion*, p. 1; *A Supplement to the Oxford English Dictionary*, 1961, s.v. "heterosexual," "homosexual"; *Tresor de la langue français*, s.v. "heterosexuel," "homosexuel."
3. For a somewhat different but not totally dissimilar treatment, see Illich, *Gender*, pp. 147, 157, discussed in Chapter 7 below.

successive defensive strategies. Synthesizing Foucault's idea that sexology constituted an intensification of control with the more commonly held notion that it constituted an extension of freedom, Chauncey seems to be suggesting that a given form of sexual science might simultaneously extend freedom and act as a defense against still more freedom.[4]

In his discussion of sexology, which he limits to the period around 1900, Chauncey focuses on the shift from a model that emphasized the distinction between normal and inverted gender to one which distinguished between heterosexual and homosexual "object-choice." What Chauncey is saying is that the first model functioned as a defense against the growing tendency of women to take an active role in social and political life by defining such activity as a masculine function and thus a symptom of "sexual inversion" when it appeared in the female. When, despite the medicalized stigmas of sexology, women continued to take an ever more active role in public life, these stigmas were revised. In the second model, women's activity was accepted, provided it was directed toward a heterosexual (and ultimately heterogenital and procreative) goal. Chauncey thus demonstrates the ambiguity implicit in sexual science.[5]

Nevertheless, Chauncey's thesis needs to be situated in a larger context, and one that will better explain the complex internal dynamics of theorization about sex. In the nineteenth century, Western medicine inherited the Enlightenment distinction between procreative and nonprocreative sex, the first "natural" and the second "unnatural" according to the criterion of reproduction as the proper end or use of sexual desire. In this context, it appeared that heterogenital intercourse was the natural function of the sexual impulse so that sexual variations were relegated to the status of errors, in the form of innocent mistakes or cultivated vices.

4. George Chauncey, "From Sexual Inversion to Homosexuality: Medicine and the Changing Conceptualization of Female Deviance," *Salmagundi* 58–59 (Fall 1982–Winter 1983), 114–46.
    5. Ibid., p. 144.

Against this background, the emergence of a Darwinism which made variation itself the heart of the evolutionary process marked a possible subversion of the sexual absolutism inherited from the Enlightenment. From Darwin on, the sexual domain became a contested field, and the science of sex emerged as a discipline torn between the absolutism of heterogenital sex on the one hand and the increasing relativization and democratization of sex on the other. It is thus possible to improve upon Chauncey's article by distinguishing *three* phases in the history of sexology during the period from 1870 to 1920, phases in which sexual science attempted to deny even as it contributed to the relativization of desire and the homogenization of the sexes implicit in the triumph of a Darwinian perspective. In the first phase (c. 1870–1895), sexology preserved the Englightenment distinction between procreative and nonprocreative desire by separating normal heterogenitality from its perverse distortions. The second phase (c. 1895–1915) distinguished between normal and inverted sexual subjects. The third phase (1915–) distinguished between the desire for heterosexual and the desire for homosexual objects. What follows is an attempt to elaborate on these phases and to explain their larger significance in the history of Western thought.[6]

I

As sexology discovered evidence of ever more complex and subtle forms of sexual variation, it became increasingly necessary to explain away these variations as distortions of the normal heterogenital impulse. At first, writers on sex accomplished this task of explanation by the widespread use of the ecological model of desire described in Chapter 2.

---

6. A more thorough discussion of how Darwin represented a radical break with older ideas about sexuality may be found in my article "Darwin and Gender."

Utilizing the idea of scarcity that articulated so much of late-nineteenth-century physics and economics, many sexologists linked high civilization to overstimulation. In this way, the emergence of the perverse could be understood as the "marginalization" of desire. Accordingly, Bloch would link "satiety" of normal heterogenitality to "the desire for sharp and novel stimulants." George Beard, the American expert on the so-called disease of neurasthenia (nervous exhaustion), associated the overstimulation of the nervous system with the excessive stimulation of normal and the consequent appearance of abnormal tastes. Within this theoretical framework, sexologists stigmatized masturbation as a vehicle for the deadening of normal appetites, in which case abnormal ones took their place. Neurasthenia thus appeared to lead to an acquired "hyperaesthesia," an enlarged sexual consciousness. Charles Féré, who, like Freud, studied with Charcot, believed that hyperaesthesia "should not be regarded as a perfecting of sensibility, but rather as a painful sensibility . . . which causes strong reactions to follow weak excitations." Havelock Ellis emphasized the supply side of the problem, suggesting that a depleted sexual energy is a determining factor in the emergence of the perverse. Ellis thus noted that "there is certainly a tendency for a morbidly feeble impulse to become inverted." Again, he linked a feeble sexual energy to the perverse where "there is no definite act to be accomplished." Ellis suggested that perversions such as sadism and masochism in particular constituted a means by which a feeble sexuality imported energy from other psychic spheres in order to accomplish the sex act. Hyperaesthesia and perversion, Ellis appeared to be arguing, were really the result of neurasthenia.[7]

But if sexologists began by linking the perverse in general

7. Beard, *Sexual Neurasthenia*, p. 107; Féré, *Sexual Instinct*, p. 117; Ellis and Symonds, *Sexual Inversion*, pp. 41, 108; Havelock Ellis, *Studies in the Psychology of Sex* (Philadelphia: F. A. Davis, 1904), vol. 3, pt. 2, pp. 56–161, esp. pp. 140–41. Ellis's ecological explanations of sadism and masochism are discussed especially well in Robinson, *Modernization of Sex*, pp. 22–25.

to the marginalization of sexuality, they often linked specific perversions to fetishism. Such writers as Alfred Binet in France and Albert von Schrenck-Notzing in Germany made the study of fetishism the model for the investigation of all abnormal sexual phenomena in the first phase of the development of sexology.[8] For Binet, love between members of the same sex, sadism, masochism, and other so-called perversions were merely different forms of fetishism resulting from some chance incident or mental association. One objection to the fetishism model was that such chance incidents and mental associations were numerous while perverts were not. To overcome this difficulty, Binet postulated a distinction between a normal and a perverse sexual ecology. It was only in people endowed with the latter predisposition that chance incidents could generate the perverse. In this scheme, the nature of the incident merely determines the form perversion will take in the predisposed individual. Along the same lines, Schrenck-Notzing suggested that "a pathological nervous system is usually more easily and intensely impressed." According to Schrenck-Notzing, even if accidental associations determine the shape of the perversion, the capacity to be affected by these accidental associations is found only in those who "have *lost the power to compensate* the *pathological stimulus* by means of the experiences of physiological [normal] sexual life" and in those who "have *never possessed* it [that power], as in hereditary weak-mindedness." Thus, Binet and Schrenck-Notzing really evolved a system of congenitally determined sexuality in which one inherited either the predisposition to normal (physiological) or the predisposition to perverse (pathological) sexuality. Yet the latter could still be dismissed as a *diseased* distortion of a normal and natural nervous system.[9]

In contrast, Freud at first moved away from a reliance on

8. See Foucault, *History of Sexuality*, p. 154.

9. Binet, "Fétichisme dans l'amour," pp. 164–67; Albert von Schrenck-Notzing, *Therapeutic Suggestion in Psychopathia Sexualis*, trans. Charles Chaddock (Philadelphia: F. A. Davis, 1895), pp. 154–55.

hereditary predisposition because he emphasized a form of chance incident whose associations would be so traumatic that they would be sufficient in themselves to distort the natural sex impulse. In his famous—or infamous—"seduction theory," Freud argued that the genesis of perversion and related neuroses could be found only in the actual seduction of children by adults. Indeed, the term "seduction" is quite misleading in this context because Freud clearly assumed that children had *no* sexuality. According to his argument, even when children did exhibit a kind of sexual drive by, say, seducing another child, the seducing child must have originally been seduced by an adult.[10] So perversion (under which Freud in effect subsumed childhood sexuality) created not only neurosis but also more perversion. According to the seduction theory, perversion could have its genesis only in earlier perversion. Freud's early theory, then, tended to treat the perverse as a type of unnatural reality whose only origin was past unreality. By assuming a natural heterogenital need and assigning the genesis of the perversion of that need to contact with previously perverted seducers, the seduction theory effectively denied (much as Binet and Schrenck-Notzing denied) the *ultimate* reality of the perverse. Moreover, Freud's seduction theory tended to restrict its conception of active sexuality to adult males, excluding women (implicitly) and children (explicitly) from the sexual and thus the social order.[11]

In short, the so-called environmentalist theories characteristic of what I have chosen to call the first phase of sexology were really not environmentalist at all except when it came to the perverse. On the contrary, these theories took as self-evident the inborn nature of heterogenitality as a species or universal need. But, by admitting the possibility and the extent of perversion, the early sexologists began to subvert this

10. Sigmund Freud, "Heredity and the Aetiology of the Neuroses," "Further Remarks on the Neuro-Psychoses of Defense," and "The Aetiology of Hysteria," all in *Standard Edition* 3:141–224, especially pp. 155, 169, 207.

11. *Standard Edition* 3:152–56, 163–74, 202–9.

very idea of a natural exclusive heterogenitality. If acquired perverse sexuality could be traced back to the distortion of natural heterogenitality under conditions of hyperaesthesia, as Bloch maintained, the widespread character of this distortion could hardly be denied. Similarly, the seduction theory explained how perversion might proliferate even as that same theory stigmatized the perverse as unreal. Binet and Schrenck-Notzing actually went a step further by implying the existence of a specific organic predisposition to the perverse even though they stigmatized that predisposition as a pathological distortion of the natural nervous system.[12]

II

Freud's controversial abandonment of the seduction theory in the last few years of the nineteenth century, whatever it meant to him personally, exemplified a general trend in sexology. For Freud, the abandonment of the seduction theory led to the acceptance of the Oedipus complex, which was nothing less than a counterseduction theory. When Freud gave up the hypothesis that children were being seduced, he replaced it with the hypothesis that children were doing the seducing (if only in the realm of fantasy). The adoption of the Oedipus complex signaled Freud's acceptance of a universal individualism. Previously Freud had regarded children as sexless victims. But Freud's subsequent sexualization of children (like that of women) conferred a kind of symbolic citizenship upon them. In this context, the new stress on fantasy that appeared with the introduction of the Oedipus complex, far from being a repudiation of reality, was actually an expression of the radically idiosyncratic character of desire itself. Freud's abandonment of the seduction theory in favor of the Oedipus complex thus symbolized his abandonment of the idea of sex as social need in fa-

12. Binet, "Fétichisme dans l'amour," pp. 164–67.

vor of the idea of sex as individualistic desire rooted in the radically idiosyncratic organic constitution of each person. Freud had begun with a general theory opposing hetero-genital to perverse sexuality, and in abandoning the seduc-tion theory, he did not fully discard his original dichotomi-zation. But whereas he had previously rooted the origin of the perverse in trauma, he now saw that origin in the underdevelopment of the genital zone. At first glance, the new theory appears to be simply a reformulation of the idea of the perverse as an abolition or negation of normal sex. Once again, perversion appears to be a distortion (false con-sciousness) of heterogenitality. But in the new conception of desire which fueled the Oedipus complex, Freud under-stood the weakness of the genital zone only in comparison to the strength of the other erogenous zones. The very exis-tence of these zones gave perversion a positive or real foun-dation. This new emphasis on the reality of perversion, con-ditioned by the gradual triumph of a Darwinian monism, tended to rupture desire from reproduction.[13]

As soon as perversion was solidly and positively rooted in evolutionary theory, it tended to banish the primacy of heterogenitality, and, with it, the idea of an exclusively paternal sexuality. When all sexuality became perversely emancipated from reproduction and everyone became sexu-alized, a new way of distinguishing normal from abnormal sex was required. In a sense, evolutionary theory contrived to solve the problem it had created by replacing the distinc-tion between normal and distorted sexuality with a distinc-tion between advanced and primitive sexuality. As soon as sexologists recognized the reality of the perverse, they be-

13. For an alternative view of Freud's abandonment of the seduction theory, see Jeffrey M. Masson, *The Assault on Truth: Freud's Suppression of the Seduction Theory* (New York: Farrar, Straus & Giroux, 1984), discussed below in Chapter 7. For the emergence of Freud's conception of the perverse, see Freud, *Origins of Psychoanalysis*, pp. 100, 147, 177, 178–80, 185–86, 215–16, 231–32; Laplanche and Pontalis, *Language of Psycho-Analysis*, s.v. "perver-sion," p. 308.

gan to stigmatize it as primitive. In the new evolutionary
conception of sex, "advanced" meant differentiated and
"backward" undifferentiated. Sexologists postulated the descent of humanity from a primeval asexual organism whose
erogenous zone stretched over its whole body. The history
of the world was, consequently, the history of its sexual differentiation. Armed with this conception, sexologists could
dismiss woman's sexuality, childhood sexuality, and perverse sexuality as remnants of a more primitive epoch. But
in this new paradigm of sexual science, the focus shifted
from the stigmatization of perversion, the reality of which
was now conceded, to the stigmatization of undifferentiated
sexual characteristics. Sexologists began with the assumption that attraction to the female was a fully differentiated
masculine characteristic and attraction to the male was a
fully differentiated female one. It followed that attraction to
one's own sex was by definition not only an "inversion" of
sex but a remnant or a reappearance of the original undifferentiated sexuality.

The way the study of inversion now ousted that of fetishism as the central focus of sexology is illustrated by the
widely copied nosology developed by Krafft-Ebing. In a
sense, this senior colleague of Freud at Vienna was the real
founder of sexual science. Just as countless minor nineteenth-century intellectuals wrote a "political economy," so
countless early-twentieth-century students of sex must have
fantasized about writing a "psychopathia sexualis." Before
1900, Krafft-Ebing had become the grand old man of the
study of sex by relying on a synthetic approach. Highly
eclectic, he absorbed many different opinions into his *Psychopathia*, and constantly revised it. But at the center of the
loosely constructed system were some fundamental assumptions that both shaped and were shaped by the prevailing
ideology. Krafft-Ebing's recognition that masculinity and
femininity had a common origin mandated that he regard
them as a matter of degree. Accordingly, he arranged his
cases of sexual inversion or intermediacy into a series of

transitional types. In the normal activity of the male and the passivity of the female, he perceived the germs of, respectively, a sadistic and a masochistic constitution.[14] Consequently masochism in the male and sadism in the female appeared to be partial inversions.[15] A more complete inversion, the first in a whole series of transitional types, was the psychical hermaphrodite in whom "by the side of the pronounced sexual instinct and the desire for the same sex, a desire toward the opposite sex is present." Even more inverted was the so-called "urning," whose desire, Krafft-Ebing explained, is directed toward his (her) own sex exclusively, but whose "anomaly is limited to the sexual life, and does not more deeply and seriously affect character and mental personality." But reversal or transposition of sexuality, so Krafft-Ebing would maintain, was still more evidenced among the "fully developed cases in which males are females in feeling; and *vice versa* women, males." Indeed, in these cases "the boy likes to spend his time with girls, play with dolls, and help his mother about the house." Finally, according to Krafft-Ebing's system, there was the totally inverted individual who "approaches the opposite sex anthropologically, and in more than a psychical or psychosexual way." Subsumed under the rubric of incompletely differentiated sexuality were thus a multiplicity of disparate transvestitisms, transsexualities, effeminacies, and homosexualities that twentieth-century scientists would gradually come to recognize as radically separate phenomena.[16]

Accepting the reality of perversion, the second phase of sexology none the less continued to deny the ultimate reality of inversion by implying that the sexual drive was always heterosexual. Sex was always a matter of male and female, the argument went. If the male was attracted to other males, his was really a "feminine" soul in a male body; if the female was attracted to other females, hers was really a "mascu-

14. Krafft-Ebing, *Psychopathia Sexualis*, pp. 137–38.
15. Ibid.; Robinson, *Modernization of Sex*, pp. 22–25.
16. Krafft-Ebing, *Psychopathia Sexualis*, pp. 231, 240, 253, 258.

line" soul in a female body. Sexologists were really saying that inverted love was normal love manifesting itself in an abnormal physiology. They believed that the normal heterosexual instinct shone through an abnormal organic prism. Thus, Havelock Ellis concluded that there was "a tendency for the invert to be attracted to persons unlike himself." According to this conception of things, the more inverted or masculine woman seeks out the relatively less inverted and comparatively feminine woman for her lover, while the more inverted or effeminate man seeks out the relatively less inverted and comparatively masculine man for his companion. But what did the sexologists make of all this? If desire for the male was characteristic of the female and desire for the female was characteristic of the male, then the differentiation of the sexes had to culminate in an exclusive heterosexuality. Sexual theorists thus concluded that the invert retains traces of an earlier "bisexuality" in which the masculine attraction to the female was not yet differentiated from the feminine attraction to the male. In this conception of bisexuality, the invert is conceived of as undifferentiated, experiencing the heterosexual drive of the male toward the female and the heterosexual drive of the female toward the male simultaneously.[17]

Despite what appeared to be an impregnable argument against the ultimate reality of anything but male-female love, however, the inversion model contained the seeds of a further disintegration of bourgeois normality. First, if male inverts were to be stigmatized it was necessary to define desire for the male as feminine. But this implied that it was normal, after all, for women to desire actively.[18] Second, a literal interpretation of inversion as a return to a less differ-

17. Ellis and Symonds, *Sexual Inversion*, pp. 37–39, 118–19. For an interesting restatement of the "intermediate" theory, see the curious work by "Xavier Mayne," *The Intersexes: A History of Similisexualism as a Problem of Social Life* (Printed privately in 1908; rpt. New York: Arno, 1975).
18. See Isabel Hull, "The Bourgeoisie and Its Discontents: Reflections on 'Nationalism and Respectability,'" *Journal of Contemporary History* 17 (1982), 261–65.

entiated stage logically precluded an explanation of exclusive desire for the same sex. After all, if a differentiated male was by definition attracted only to women, and a differentiated female was attracted only to men, then an undifferentiated individual must be attracted to both. Confronted with the logical impossibility of explaining *exclusive* desire for the same sex, Krafft-Ebing and his followers increasingly insisted on explanations providing for the independent differentiation of various tissues. For example, in the case of the male invert, it was proposed that the "psychosexual" center of the brain might differentiate fully in the female direction, generating an exclusive desire for the male, while the sexual glands might differentiate fully in the male direction, conditioning the development of an unmistakably male body. Sexologists increasingly spoke of a male brain in a female body or a female brain in a male body, without being very convincing even to themselves. But, in 1893, Julien Chevalier emphasized the struggle within the embryo "between male and female elements, resulting in the triumph of one or the other" in normally differentiated individuals.[19] Havelock Ellis, several years later, seemed to adhere to this theory in his classic, *Sexual Inversion*, reasoning that "as development proceeds either the male or the female germs assume the upper hand" in the process of sexual differentiation. The failure of one or the other to dominate led to inversion. Here, inversion no longer appeared a reversion to an earlier stage but a variation "in the present stage of evolution," thus affording a way of conceptually separating the invert from the primitive. More significantly, the postulation of the invert as a kind of sexual "mosaic" may have offered a clearer explanation for exclusive homosexuality, but it also further diluted what holism remained in sexology. The increasing emphasis on the idiosyncratic, chance character of sex differentiation, of ontogeny over phylogeny

19. See Julien Chevalier, *Une maladie de la personalité: L'inversion sexuelle* (Lyons: Storck, 1893), pp. 410–11.

and teratology over heredity, signaled a movement in the direction of greater individualism.[20]

III

The theories discussed above attempted to explain all sexuality in terms of male and female. According to this conception, masculinity and femininity appeared to be the irreducible elements of sex, and all desire was heterosexual. But some sexologists, especially after the turn of the century, began to recognize that it was not always possible to resolve apparent homosexual attraction comfortably into an underlying attraction between male and female elements. Havelock Ellis, for one, had to admit that sometimes in relations "between men . . . the invert cannot tell if he feels like a man or like a woman." Again, Freud's one-time rival Albert Moll took note of the "'real' Uranists [homosexuals] whom aside from their sexual perversion act in everything else as men." In surveying the classification scheme employed by Krafft-Ebing, Moll noted its failure to account for "certain forms of very acute effeminacy" in which "men whose entire manner of acting recalled that of women . . . had intercourse only with women, and who found complete satisfaction therein."[21]

Another attempt to understand the elusive phenomenon of homosexuality was made by the French writer Marc Raffalovich. In an article published in 1895 in the *Journal of Comparative Neurology*, Raffalovich wrote: "The inverts are not at all content with the old explanation of the feminine soul in the masculine body. Some of them are more masculine than other men and are attracted to their own sex in

20. Ellis and Symonds, *Sexual Inversion*, pp. 105–6, 133–37; Krafft-Ebing, *Psychopathia Sexualis*, pp. 226–27.

21. Ellis and Symonds, *Sexual Inversion*, p. 118; Albert Moll, *Perversions of the Sex Instinct: A Study of Sexual Inversion Based on Clinical Data and Official Documents* (New York: AMS Press, 1976), pp. 75–77, 138–39.

proportion to the resemblance. They say they despise women too much to be effeminate. Others think that similarity is a passion comparable to that excited by sexual dissimilarity. As men, they love men; but they affirm that if they were women, they would love women."[22] I believe that Raffalovich here provided an adumbration of the long-term trend of sexology. Neither the first nor the second style of sexology provided a model of sexuality that could adequately meet the objections of his informants who emphasized a type of desire based on sameness (literally homosexuality). It was not until the second decade of the twentieth century that this kind of desire began to be systematically explored.

The conception of the invert as an "intermediate" or partially differentiated form had been an article of faith during the second phase of sexology. But in his *Intermediate Types among Primitive Folk*, Edward Carpenter contrasted the "sex-types that may be called truly intermediate" with "types quite beyond the normal at either end of the scale— namely the *super-virile* man and the *ultra-feminine* woman." It was the latter types that Carpenter would link to what he called "comrade-love" among peers, or love between similars. But although Carpenter here grasped a kind of desire which appears radically different because it cannot be reduced to a *lack* of differentiation, he did not give up the differentiation model itself. On the contrary, he merely turned that model against conventional sexuality by formulating a kind of homosexuality *so* differentiated that heterosexuality appeared primitive by comparison.[23]

But from 1910 to 1914 it was Freud and his followers who

22. Marc Raffalovich, "Uranism: Congenital Sexual Inversion," *Journal of Comparative Neurology* 5 (1895), 35.

23. Edward Carpenter, *Intermediate Types among Primitive Folk: A Study in Social Evolution* (New York: Arno, 1975; rpt. of 1919 ed.), pp. 87–91, 161–74. It would be interesting to read Carpenter in the context of the shift described by Chauncey; see Chauncey, "From Sexual Inversion to Homosexuality," pp. 122–23. See also Havelock Ellis, "Sexo-Aesthetic Inversion," *Alienist and Neurologist* 34 (1913), 249–79. For a discussion of the conservative character of the inversion hypothesis, see Guy Hocquenghem, *Homo-*

finally conceptualized a new type of desire. At that time, Freud's formulation of the concept of narcissism permitted the construction of a theory that could account for homosexuality as a desire between similars, thus beginning a new phase in the history of sexology. Freud regarded narcissism as the original desire, at first entirely invested in the self-contained world of the subject. Modified by experience, the individual withdraws that desire from itself and invests it in others as a means of ultimately satisfying its self-desire and self-preservation. This thesis in itself was not particularly innovative, even at the time. The real innovation was Freud's hypothesis that desire for others might direct itself to two very different kinds of love objects, one based on our "own selves" and the other on our mothers. By linking the classification of sexualities to the theory of narcissism, Freud was apparently able to construct a system of distinctions all the more remarkable because this system did not appear to be directly grounded in gender at all. The duality between the love of sameness and the love of differentness appeared to be more fundamental than the distinction between male and female. Moreover, same-sexuality (homosexuality) and different-sexuality (heterosexuality) appeared if only for a fleeting moment to be equal in value because they were both directed outward to full objects.[24]

Still, much of the radicality of this theory remained only implicit. The potential equality of heterosexuality and homosexuality was subverted by the latter's more intimate connection to the original self-love. Thus, the new theory could be reduced, if only indirectly, to the old evolutionary

---

sexual Desire, trans. Daniella Dangoor (London: Allison & Busby, 1978), pp. 107–13. It must still be remembered, however, that from the perspective of the doctrines of seduction theory and other remnants of the first phase the post-Darwinian conceptualizations of the inversion hypothesis may be described as radical. For a criticism of the work of Magnus Hirschfeld, see Martin Dennecker, Theories of Homosexuality, trans. David Fernbach (London: Gay Men's Press, 1981). I have tended to ignore Hirschfeld, who became increasingly influential in the 1920s, because his early work is rather inaccessible to English-speaking readers.

24. See Freud, "On Narcissism," passim.

or pseudoevolutionary doctrine of sexual differentiation. Moreover, homosexual desire now appeared contradictory because Freud suggested that it was a compromise between an interest in oneself and an interest in an external object. Indeed, according to Guy Hocquenghem, "by making his anaclitic choice on a narcissistic basis, the homosexual is in a way deprived of an object" by psychoanalytic theory.[25] If, from an evolutionary perspective, homosexuality was a link to the primitive narcissism originally rooted in the asexual mode of reproduction, from an ecological perspective, homosexuality appeared to require the withdrawal of less narcissism from the self than did heterosexuality.

As if this were not enough, Freud had already further analyzed this narcissistic desire into even more familiar components by resolving it into a type of regression or fixation brought about by overidentification with the mother. Thus, the love of sameness, grasped for an instant in all its radicality, collapsed back into a distortion of the universal love of differentness founded on the relationship with the mother. To be sure, however, this process of analysis became increasingly complex, especially because the mother was the original external object for *both* sexes. The more the radically polymorphous and idiosyncratic character of sex was recognized, the more difficult it became to explain it away. Freud successfully stigmatized narcissism as primitive, but it could just as easily serve (as Herbert Marcuse would argue) as the basis for an undeniably different and rival sexuality.[26]

IV

I have been arguing that during the late nineteenth century and the early twentieth three phases or styles of

25. Hocquenghem, *Homosexual Desire*, p. 68.
26. See Sigmund Freud, *Leonardo Da Vinci and a Memory of His Childhood*, trans. Alan Tyson (New York: Norton, 1964), p. 49; Herbert Marcuse, *Eros and Civilization* (Boston: Beacon, 1974), passim.

sexology evolved in rapid succession. These theories functioned to deny, even as they exemplified, the trend toward the homogenization of the sexes and the dissolution of heterogenital hegemony. The first style of theorizing, inheriting the ideology of the previous epoch most directly, distinguished normal coitus from its distortions, thus insisting upon the primacy of heterogenital desire. The second phase differentiated between heterosexuals in the right and heterosexuals in the wrong (inverted) bodies, consequently postulating the existence of heterosexual desire alone, although it was not necessarily directed toward reproduction. But in the third phase of the early development of sexology, some sex theorists began grudgingly to admit the possibility of a homosexual as well as a heterosexual desire, thus assuming the existence only of desire in general. In other words, even as the sphere allotted to desire was enlarged, ever newer divisions and classifications of desire were constructed, thus reinstating order and hierarchy. Sexology thus appears to have functioned in part as a kind of cultural defense against its own tendency to enlarge the sphere allotted to desire.

Still, the history of sexology should be regarded as a history of transitional stage rather than one of abrupt mutations. The view I am developing is definitely opposed to bifurcating the history of sexology by linking it to some dramatic event such as the "passing of degeneration theory" (Sulloway) or the emancipation of the sexual object from the sexual instinct (Chauncey). Rather, I would stress the ongoing, gradual, and incomplete nature of these processes. For one thing, the complexity of degeneration theory is too often forgotten. I noted (in Chapter 3), for example, the use of the threefold distinction between morbid, atavistic and, atypical degeneration, the first associated with the deathlike abolition of function, the second with a return to an earlier function, and the third with simple deviation. It was in the context of a shifting and complex stigmatization of variation that the successive forms of sexology introduced progressively less severe conceptions of degeneration. Thus, in the first phase, perversion was in effect stigmatized as a "morbid" dissolution of sexuality, whereas in the second phase inversion was regarded more benignly as an "atavistic" return to an older form of sexuality, and in the third phase homosexuality was increasingly treated as a relatively advanced but deviant sexuality. This process continued until, with Kinsey, homosexuality appeared merely a statistical variation from the norm, a status that nonetheless retained a residue of stigma.[27]

Again, the emancipation of the sexual instinct from the sexual object cannot be associated with any one phase in the history of sexology, but was instead symbolic of a long-term tendency in the history of that science. I have suggested that this tendency involved both the dissolution of the idea of heterogenitality as a natural need and the disintegration of the concept of a paternal monopoly of desire. These trends, accompanied by the tendency of selected perversions to escape serious stigmatization and the conceptualization of homosexuality as atypical variation, added up to the increasing differentiation of individual desire from familial and social obligations. Albert Moll had stated the classic argument when he reasoned that inversion could not be considered healthy because the definition of health embraced the social (reproductive) as well as the individualistic (self-preservative) functions.[28] Conversely, the movement toward a conception of a "healthy homosexual," obvious as early as Krafft-Ebing's last scheme, indicated the emergence of a radically idiosyncratic definition of health that might fairly be called "consumerist."

Finally, one can achieve a fuller understanding of the his-

27. For the relationship between regression, atavism, dissolution, and other forms of degeneration, see Chapters 3 and 4 above as well as Ellis and Symonds, *Sexual Inversion*, pp. 133–37, and Féré, *Sexual Instinct*, pp. 39–42, 286–87. Féré in particular regarded perversion as a breakdown of sexual function rather than a return to an earlier sexual function, so that his ideas fall more within the first than the second style of sexual theorizing I have delineated in this chapter.

28. Moll, *Perversions*, pp. 179–82.

tory of sexology by more explicitly situating it in the model I proposed in the Introduction. It is possible, I argued, to delineate the two different ideologies, one "productivist" and the other "consumerist," that dwell within sexology. This book has linked the first ideology to an Enlightenment complex of values emphasizing work, gender, and need, and the second ideology to an emerging complex of values stressing pleasure, genderlessness, and desire. Moreover, the preceding chapters have attempted to make plain the contradictions within sexual science as an expression of that science's suspension between these two ideologies. It is now possible to nuance this model. Thus, it becomes apparent that germs of the consumerist ideology appeared even in the first phase of the history of sexology, where the stigmatization of the perverse signaled an emerging emphasis on the problematic of desire. But the assumption that only the heterogenital drive was inborn and that it was paternal property illustrates the way this phase of sexology retained a substantial remnant of the older ideology, too. The "consumerist" trend was more vigorously expressed in the second phase of sexology, solidly founded on an evolutionary theory that implied the existence of an idiosyncratic and genderless sexuality. But these conceptions remained only partially emancipated because evolutionary theory was itself ambivalent toward them. In the second phase, the recognition of individualistic desire contradicted the idea of the primacy of heterogenitality, just as the recognition of the active sexuality of women and children contradicted the idea of their passivity. In the third phase, however, the homogenization of sexual *subjects*, implied by the postulation of a truly idiosyncratic, genderless, narcissistic desire, and concretized in the Freudian conceptions of a genderless libido and id, seemed to abolish the last remnant of gender and the bourgeois social order itself. It was in this context that the categories of heterosexuality and homosexuality emerged as ways of distinguishing the gender of sexual *objects*. Heterosexuality and homosexuality indeed appear to embody the last possible trace of gender and species need. In this third phase of sexology, gender is alive only in the distinction between sexual organs and body types, need only in the rudimentary hierarchy of heterosexual over homosexual desire. Heterosexuality and homosexuality are the categories sexology proposed as the latest defense against the dissolution of bourgeois values.

CHAPTER SIX

Society and Sexology

The foregoing chapters have attempted to delineate the structure and contradictions of the science of sex as it emerged in the latter part of the nineteenth century, without doing much speculation about the social context in which this emergence took place. To many intellectual historians this approach will be quite acceptable. Certainly, social context cannot in itself explain the appearance of particular values and ideas. We have the right to be skeptical of mechanistic schemes that treat intellectual phenomena simply as the reflex of material development. Yet I think we should be equally wary of these other schemes that treat ideas as self-determined phenomena, rupturing them from the rest of social history. Ideas are after all artifacts of and thus part of the culture that produces them. Moreover, the material presented in the preceding chapters suggests that sexology, like economic thought before it, was in part a way of conceptualizing society. If this is true, then it might not be inappropriate to suspect some connection between the emergence of sexual science as a new model of society and some shift in the actual structure of that society. The shift might not have to be a big one in order to provoke the appearance of a new ideology; intellectuals may tend to conceptualize far broader and more comprehensive changes than actually occur in the real world, where the quantity and quality of change may vary from place to place and from group to group.[1] Moreover, it would appear that sexual science simultaneously conceptualized *two* social structures, one representing what society had been and one representing what society was tending to become. If this was the case, it can be argued that sexology (again, like classical economics) must be understood as a symbolic representation of social change.

Fortunately, historians have extensively documented the shifts in technological and cultural structures during the period from 1871 to 1914. According to Stuart Chase, it was a period that witnessed the end of "scarcity" and the beginning of "abundance." For Geoffrey Barraclough, the years around 1890 marked the ebbing of "modern" and the emergence of "contemporary" civilization. More recently, Donald Lowe has posited a shift from developmentalist to a synchronistic "epistemic order" associated with transformations in technology about this time. It is in this context that we should put the transition from a productivist to a consumerist complex of values, a transition evidenced in the contradictions of sexual science.[2]

Historians sometimes conceptualize this transition in terms of a shift from early to late capitalism. This terminology is useful only if we are careful to characterize "early" capitalism as essentially protoindustrial rather than industrial and "late" capitalism as industrial rather than postindustrial. This is a requirement of something more than semantics. As I argued in the Introduction, we must depart from the conventional wisdom of both Marxist and moderni-

1. I am suggesting that Freud and his fellow sexologists were generously endowed with what Ronald Meek called "that peculiar feature of genius which sometimes allows it not only to observe what is typical, but also to discern and analyze what is *becoming* typical." See Ronald Meek, ed., *Turgot on Progress, Sociology and Economics* (New York: Cambridge University Press, 1973), p. 20.

2. See Chase, *Economy of Abundance*; Geoffrey Barraclough, *Introduction to Contemporary History* (New York: Penguin, 1967), pp. 9–41; Lowe, *History of Bourgeois Perception*, p. 15.

zation theorists who tend to conflate modernity, capitalism, and industrialization. Although the question of modernity is only indirectly relevant to my concern here, it is essential that we at least distinguish between capitalism and industrialization if we are to grasp the characteristics of the early capitalist period, extending from the mid-seventeenth to the mid-nineteenth century.[3] In general, recent work by social historians has stressed two important points about this period; on the one hand, how long protoindustrial technologies survived, and on the other hand, how innovative and advanced these technologies really were. For example, as early as the latter half of the eighteenth century and before the coming of the steam revolution, Europe's per-capita energy resources may have been twice those of China.[4] This advanced protoindustrial technology, which should not be confused with preindustrial technologies outside the West, was associated with a tendency toward innovation which appeared in the West very early in the form of the clock, the printing press, and the gun.[5]

We can hazard a guess that this particularly Occidental hospitality to invention was connected to the unique system of competitive states that emerged from the decentralized polities of Western Europe by the sixteenth century. This system put increasing stress on the rationalization of resources within each state. The long-term result was formalized, as we have seen, in the writings of the mercantilists in which economic growth was first conceptualized as a means of strengthening the competitive edge of the ruler and his army by increasing taxable wealth. Here was a possible origin of the ideological stress on the property owner as

3. Stoianovich and Braudel, for example, seem to conflate modernity and Western culture as a whole. See Stoianovich, *French Historical Method*, pp. 177–78.

4. Ibid., pp. 70–77; Stoianovich, "Theoretical Implications of Braudel's *Civilisation matérielle*," *Journal of Modern History* 41 (March 1969), p. 76.

5. See especially Carl Cipolla, *Before the Industrial Revolution: European Society and Economy, 1000–1700* (New York: Norton, 1976).

citizen and property as value. Locke's idea of property was further transformed or "improved" in the work of Quesnay and Smith, who both grasped the essence of capital as that property which creates more property.[6]

Neither Quesnay nor Smith conceptualized an industrial society, but they did advocate a productivist or capitalist one. Neither could envision the coming of steam power, mass production, consumerism, and advertising, but they understood the idea of improvement and they had the model of the machine in the form of the time-piece. In other words, the emphasis in early capitalism was not on rapid transformation but on slow, steady improvement. Yet in saying this we should not miss the radicality of this idea of improvement and progress. Diffused throughout transatlantic intellectual circles by the latter half of the nineteenth century, it was the cornerstone of the productivist worldview. Once the idea of improvement was tied to the emergence of the competitive state, it is not surprising enlightened despots and Enlightenment intellectuals alike would seek to remove all the impediments to the maximization of wealth available to the state. Within this context, eighteenth-century thinkers developed the notion that the state must be cleared of all the messy remnants of feudalism, all the internal barriers bequeathed by the past which stood in the way of a free movement of property owners and their property. In this sense, Ricardo and Rousseau are two sides of the same coin. The effect of these ideas, beginning with Hobbes, was to provide a rationale for the emancipation of the property-owning citizen from the older regime of aristocratic citizens.[7]

The complex of values I have characterized as productivist

6. For the emergence of economics out of politics, see Dumont, *Essays on Individualism*, pp. 104–13.

7. In particular, I would compare Smith's demand for a free circulation of goods within the state to Rousseau's demand for a state within which there are no ties of dependency between citizens. See Rousseau, *The Social Contract*, ed. Charles Frankel (New York: Hafner, 1947), Book I, Chap. IV.

emerged in the context of a capitalist but protoindustrial culture in the course of the seventeenth and eighteenth centuries. In a sense, Marx elaborated the last and the greatest of the productivist ideologies. In providing a critique of the political economists who preceded him, Marx ended up looking back rather than ahead, becoming trapped in the very ideology he criticized. His system really preserved a remnant of the cultural assumptions of the bourgeois epoch, assumptions upon which he erected a titanic structure. If we distinguish between an era of protoindustrial technology associated with a developmentalist perspective and a later era of industrial technology associated with the passing of developmentalism, we may quite properly locate Marx in the former period. Thus, at the same time that his philosophy upheld the Enlightenment ideas of improvement and productivity, that philosophy took its stand against the machine in a fundamental way. I am talking here not about Marx's opinion of the effect of machinery, but about the much more subtle doctrine of human labor as the source of all value. In effect, Marx defined production as a purely human activity, holding that machines create no new value that has not been put in them already by their creators. For Marx, the machine cannot create anything. But, just as significantly, human beings are capable of true creation through labor. In the deepest sense, then, Marxism symbolizes the paradox of an ideology constructed during an epoch that simultaneously glorified production and still remained fundamentally protoindustrial.[8]

But even as Marx wrote, this epoch was coming to a close. Early capitalism had emphasized the building up of infra-

8. My discussion of the labor theory of value is based on my readings in the first volume of Marx's *Capital*. For a popular and quite useful outline of the implications of the Marxian theory of value, see David McLellan, *Karl Marx* (New York: Penguin, 1975), pp. 49–61; for an examination of Marx's and Engels's attitude toward machinery and technology in general, see John Sherwood, "Engels, Marx, Malthus, and the Machine," *American Historical Review* 90 (October 1985), 837–65.

structure and other "macroeconomic" tasks, first as a means of strengthening the ruler and his army and then as an end in themselves. On that basis, classical political economy began with production, emphasizing reinvestment and growth instead of personal consumption. In the course of the nineteenth century, the culminative effect of this emphasis on production and progress was a series of startling breakthroughs in technology; steam, rail, telegraph, electricity, and steel were the prerequisites for an industrial mass culture that began to appear in widely dispersed areas in both Western Europe and North America. The acceleration in the expansion of productive capacity, registered by the amount of energy available to each individual, was signaled by the gradual amelioration of mass poverty after 1850. Although this trend was gradual and should not be overemphasized, it was real and probably bound up with the exigencies of an industrializing mass economy. Certainly it was widespread. For example, in France, personal income among Parisian workers increased about 65 percent in the two generations after 1850. It was not much different in Britain, according to W. H. Fraser, or in the newly unified German Empire and United States.[9]

The development in productive capacity and technology was registered in a shift toward the production of consumer goods and in a new emphasis on "microeconomics." New technologies in metallurgy and chemistry made possible the mass production of an increasing variety of necessarily low-

9. See W. Hamish Fraser, *The Coming of the Mass Market, 1850–1914* (London: Archon, 1981), pp. 27, 66–82; David Landes, *The Unbound Prometheus: Technological Change and Industrial Development in Western Europe from 1750 to the Present* (Cambridge: Cambridge University Press, 1977), pp. 241–48; William R. Leach, "Transformations in a Culture of Consumption: Women and Department Stores, 1890–1925," *Journal of American History* 71 (September 1984); Gustav Stolper, *The German Economy: 1870 to the Present* (New York: Harcourt, Brace & World, 1967), p. 21; Rosalind Williams, *Dream Worlds: Mass Consumption in Late Nineteenth Century France* (Berkeley: University of California Press, 1984), pp. 9–10.

cost household goods.[10] The advent of the bicycle in particular was emblematic of this democratization of goods in the late nineteenth century. First appearing between 1870 and 1880, the bicycle, even more than the automobile, which followed it some years later, marked a rupture with the past and the beginning of a new social order. Not only did the lowly cycle make wide-spread a mobility unavailable even to aristocrats of the previous epoch, but this invention also made possible a partial emancipation of women and children from paternal supervision. Like an automobile, the bicycle demonstrated the way mass production and consumption could disrupt the power of adults over children and men over women by democratizing space, thus necessitating newer and perhaps more subtle forms of control, which took the shape of ideology. By 1900, there were five million bicycles in Britain, five million in France, and four million in Germany.[11]

The emergence of the bicycle is also a significant indicator of a new stress on leisure, entertainment, and the body toward the end of the nineteenth century. The beginnings of "sport" can probably be dated from this period. In his account of the evolution of modern sports, Benjamin Rader has suggested that since 1890 organized athletics moved from a "player-centered" (production-oriented?) to a "spectator-centered" (consumer-oriented?) mode. Even if this is true, from its late-nineteenth-century beginnings sport was associated with a new stress on spectacle, sensation, and play. In this sense, sport has always been a highly ambivalent enterprise, embodying both productivist and consumerist values, upholding masculinity and self-discipline on the one hand and transsexuality and self-indulgence on the

10. For a discussion of the specific relationship between technology and the emergence of mass consumption, see Landes, *Unbound Prometheus*, p. 244.

11. Figures taken from Carlton Hays, *A Generation of Materialism, 1871–1900* (New York: Harper & Row, 1963), p. 90.

other. Sport as we know it indeed may survive only as long as there continues to be tension between these two value systems, disappearing with the triumph of a more purely consumerist culture.[12]

From another perspective, the increasing stress on leisure and the body reveals the ever greater emphasis put on consumption as a means to absorb the greatly increased productive capacity. This new emphasis on consumption and desire developed against the background of the great depression of the last quarter of the nineteenth century. In effect, this was a producer's rather than a consumer's depression. At the same time, the period saw a major revision in economic theorizing (described above in Chapter 1), in which the accent shifted from production to distribution and consumption. Although, production continued to be important to and was greatly improved by the emerging managerial classes, the expanding volume of the product led to what Neil Borden called a "competitive struggle for control of demand."[13] The period witnessed a spectacular growth in advertising. For example, advertising revenues increased tenfold between 1865 and 1900 in the United States. In Britain, the spread of brand names (reflected in the passage of the Trade Mark Act of 1875) registered the increased "struggle for control of demand" in that country. Indeed, throughout Western Europe and North America, the period saw numerous innovations in the field of credit designed to facilitate the increased consumption of ever greater product of industry.[14]

12. Benjamin Rader, *American Sport* (Englewood Cliffs, N.J.: Prentice-Hall, 1980), passim.; Warren Susman, *Culture as History: The Transformations of American Society in the Twentieth Century* (New York: Pantheon, 1984), pp. 143–49.

13. Neil Borden, *The Economic Effects of Advertising* (Chicago: Richard Irwin, 1942), p. 49. I am indebted to Traian Stoianovich for his insight into the possible connections between marginalism and the great depression.

14. Fraser, *Coming of the Mass Market*, p. 146; Williams, *Dream Worlds*, p. 10, for the situation in France. For American advertising, see Borden, *Economic Effects*.

It is tempting to hypothesize that the very success of productivist values in promoting growth led to a decline of those values among intellectuals once a certain level of growth was achieved. Certainly, by the end of the nineteenth century, the turn away from the idea of progress was associated with a sense that society was richer than ever before. Ortega y Gasset suggested that precisely because mass society had achieved the material (productivist?) aims of earlier societies, there was a loss of interest among intellectuals in conceptualizing further material gain. Unknowingly, perhaps, Ortega addressed the paradox of late-nineteenth-century culture: why it was only with the emergence of an "abundant" economy that the ideology of "scarcity" triumphed. Apparently, the triumph of the productvist model was *too* successful; the very success of productivism abolished the ideological preeminence of production, which gradually gave way to the new emphasis on desire. Thus, Ortega noted "the astonishing fact that these epochs of so-called plenitude have always felt in the depths of their consciousness a special form of sadness." Certainly, that sadness was indicated among intellectuals by the emergence of a pessimistic ideology of desire, succeeding the more optimistic ideology of labor.[15]

How far ideology had shifted in the last quarter of the nineteenth century is well illustrated by a comparison of Marx's productivist and Freud's quasi-consumerist philosophy. If Marx exemplified the importance of production in the classical epoch by his vision of work as an end in itself, Freud exemplified the shift toward consumption by his conception of production as a necessary means toward the ultimate goal of consumption. For Marx, work was a positive force that was both objective and creative. For Freud, in contrast, work was merely a negative deferral of play. In this sense, the reality principle was not a produc-

15. José Ortega y Gasset, *The Revolt of the Masses* (New York: Norton, 1957), p. 32.

tion principle but a substitute for a production principle. Still, Freud did not completely embrace this consumerist complex of values. Again and again, he reasserted the importance if not the primacy of work, linking (like the marginalist economists) the ability to defer pleasure to the development of civilization. Freud had a negative definition of work, but it was still a definition. If Marx stood at the end of the productivist, Freud stood only at the beginning of the consumerist tradition. In Freud, a transitional figure, the trend toward an industrial ideology of abundance was by no means fully developed, though its appearance during the opening of the age of advertising is suggestive enough. For Freud, like advertising, focused on the mechanism of desire-formation necessary to stimulate demand.[16]

It was against the background of a multiplication of consumer goods and thus (as Ortega noted) of possibilities for "mass man" that the holistic concept of use retreated before the individualistic idea of consumption as an end in itself. Under these circumstances, we have seen, neoclassical economics emancipated desire in the form of marginal utility from socially determined needs or utilities. At the same time, sexology liberated perversity from heterogenitality, redefining the meaning of "sex" in the process. This redefinition of sexuality is central to any understanding of the series of changes that have gripped Western cultures since the latter part of the nineteenth century, changes whose more recent manifestations are sometimes summed up under the term "sexual revolution."[17]

Recently published theorists such as Eli Zaretsky and Dennis Altman have attempted to situate this sexual revolution in the transition from early to late capitalism. In particular, their arguments attempt to link what I have termed the "dissolution of holism" to specific economic changes.

16. See Susman, *Culture as History*, pp. 271–85.

17. For a review of the theories linking marginalist economics to its historical context, see Mark Blaug, *Economic Theory in Retrospect* (Cambridge: Cambridge University Press, 1974), pp. 309–24.

Zaretsky and Altman, among others, have underscored the distinction between a system of exchange oriented around production, which flourished in parts of Western Europe and its North American colonies in the eighteenth and nineteenth centuries, and a system of exchange oriented around consumption, which has flourished since the late nineteenth century in what Immanuel Wallerstein has called the "core" of the "world-economy." In the earlier system, the argument goes, the protoindustrial production of capital goods took place within the (masculine) sphere of the political economy while consumer goods continued to be produced within the (feminine) sphere of the domestic economy. In the latter system, however, the extension of political economy to include the industrial production of consumer goods made the existence of a separate feminine sphere obsolete, thus encouraging the erosion of separate sexual functions as part of the trend toward consumption. This argument suggests that, even when regional, national, ethnic, and class differences are taken into account, the long-term trend in mass society toward genderlessness and the consequent dissolution of the family are the product of economic shifts.[18]

Certainly the shift from a productivist to a consumerist set of values involved a deemphasis on property in favor of credit and income-stream. As long as production was associated with the accumulation of wealth over time, family and inheritance remained important factors. Productivist culture was hardly hostile to the family, which, conceived as a

---

18. Dennis Altman, *The Homosexualization of America* (Boston: Beacon, 1982), pp. 79–107; Eli Zaretsky, *Capitalism, the Family and Personal Life* (New York: Harper & Row, 1976); John D'Emilio, "Capitalism and Gay Identity," in Ann Snitow, Christine Stansell, and Sharon Thompson, eds., *Powers of Desire* (New York: Monthly Review Press, 1983), pp. 102–4; Barry Adam, "A Social History of Gay Politics," in Martin Levine, ed., *Gay Men: The Sociology of Male Homosexuality* (New York: Harper & Row, 1979), pp. 285–300. The focus of most of this literature is on the effect of consumerism on women and gay men; less has been done on how the consumerist culture has led to a self-redefinition among heterosexual men also.

natural institution, played a vital role by augmenting the accumulation of capital at the disposal of individual property owners. Property came to play an important role in the choice of a marriage partner in the protoindustrial societies of Northern Europe and North America; this importance is apparent in the writings of Jane Austen and in Hippolyte Taine's proposal of an "agence matrimoniale universelle" designed to apply to marriage the cold logic of the stock exchange. (Yet, within marriage itelf, sentiment might reign because bourgeois society juxtaposed a masculine culture of rationality with a feminine culture of sentiment.) In Cobbett's *Advice to a Young Man* (1830), the qualities listed for a good wife included chastity, sobriety, industry, frugality, cleanliness, domestic economy, good temper, and, last only, beauty. Both bourgeois "masculine" values such as industry and bourgeois "feminine" values such as cleanliness were emphasized, and beauty listed last. Desire was, in a sense, subordinated to the needs of the family.[19]

But in the course of the nineteenth century, the emergence of an industrialized culture that shifted the emphasis toward desire, in order to assure the absorption of a greatly increased production, seems to have necessitated an increasing stress on "impulse." In this sense, a consumerist set of values may have acted (and may still be acting) to undercut the importance of property by stressing disaccumulation over accumulation. Certainly, a culture emphasizing radically idiosyncratic spending would be unlikely to retain much interest in the family as an institution for saving. How much things may have changed from 1830 to 1930 can be estimated if one compares Cobbett's *Advice* to Theodore Van der Velde's immensely popular *Ideal Marriage*. Widely circulated in the 1930s, *Ideal Marriage* argued that a good wife was a good lover, thus justifying marriage as the most satis-

19. William Cobbett, *Advice to a Young Man* (Oxford: Oxford University Press, 1980), p. 96; H. Taine, *Notes sur Paris: Vie et opinions de M. Frédéric-Thomas Graindorge* (Paris: Hatchette, 1907), pp. 162–73; this work is discussed and interpreted in Stoianovich, "Gender and Family."

fying relationship in a world of relationships. For Van der Velde, and probably for the whole type of literature he represents, desire had become the central criterion. And yet, Van der Velde was working against some manifestations of desire, those that threatened to destroy marriage and the family. To "sell" marriage, he attempted to reinforce the vanishing primacy of coitus and especially marital coitus, already threatened on a popular level in the 1920s by insisting that a good marriage and normal intercourse within it could maximize the pleasure of both partners. But by stressing desire, Van der Velde probably contributed to the diffusion of the very attitudes he was trying to preserve marriage against. In this sense, his work reproduced on a popularized level and at a later date the ambiguities present in late-nineteenth-century sexology.[20]

The transition from a protoindustrial to a mass industrial capitalism thus provided (in part at least) the social context for the emancipation of women and children as *consumers*. But this identification of consumerism with transsexuality must be qualified. Superficially at least, consumer messages (advertising) have from their inception tended to reinforce the gendered stereotypes inherited from earlier epochs. In this sense, consumerist culture has acted explicitly to preserve gender even as it has acted implicitly (and possibly more fundamentally) to erode it by treating both sexes as consumers. Nothing else so illustrates the transitional nature of the period beginning in the second half of the nineteenth century as this ambiguity. The emergence of the department store after 1850 on both sides of the Atlantic was emblematic of the contradictions between the old and the new values,

20. Theodore Hendrick Van der Velde, *Ideal Marriage: Its Physiology and Technique* (New York: Random House, c. 1930). Just as neoclassical economics has reduced itself to the role of a "technique" for satisfying the desires of the consumer, so popular "sexology" has to some extent done the same. But even popular sexologists, psychologists, and sex writers tend to retain a remnant of moralism in order to regulate the anarchic world they stimulate.

values that were expressed side by side. On the one hand, the department store drew women and even children into the public sphere by specifically appealing to their desire. On the other hand, these institutions continued to encourage segregation by sex and age through a ghettoized organization of floor space and the use of stereotyped imagery.[21]

The department stores themselves represented the convergence of trends toward consumerism and urbanization during the transition to an industrialized culture, a transition that included a redefinition of the political and social space of gender. These changes had their most immediate and dramatic effect on the upper-middle classes, and it was precisely these classes that provided the model for the generalizations about society and individuality implicit it in sexology. Broadly speaking, early capitalism was associated with the accentuation of the social and spatial distance between the sexes, at least among the propertied. This accentuation of social and spatial distance is clearly being reversed in the twentieth century, a century that has witnessed the increasing conflation of the personal and the political. In the course of the movement from a productivist to a consumerist culture, the concept of separate spheres of action for each sex began to give way to a concept of a single sphere of action. As we have seen, this movement signals the final dissolution of caste or difference, which survives only in an attenuated form as differentiation from a common sameness. In the process of this shift, the position of women began to be substantially redefined, often by women themselves. Indeed, as much of the sexological literature cited above suggests, the sexologists attributed a substantial part of the drive to alter woman's position to women. Nineteenth-century "ladies" continued to internalize the values of the "feminine" sphere by claiming truly to speak from the perspective of home and family, but these same women

21. For the ambiguity of the department store's relationship to gender, see Leach, "Transformations," pp. 321–22.

increasingly spoke from this perspective in public. In the latter decades of the nineteenth century, then, the place of the "lady" became increasingly ambiguous, vacillating between private and public, between domesticity and political involvement (often justified as a means of preserving domesticity). In this sense, the ambiguity of woman's position in sexological conceptions actually bore a real if limited resemblance to her shifting status within the bourgeois milieu.[22]

That milieu (the urbanized upper middle or middle classes) was the original cradle of the consumerist complex of values. Despite the differences that existed from one country to another, the urbanized upper-middle and middle classes of the industrializing countries on both sides of the Atlantic increasingly shared a culture and thus shared ideological assumptions. In part, this growing commonality was a product of the standardization of commodities and techniques implied by industrialization, a standardization that in turn depended on the quantum leaps in transportation and communication achieved in the nineteenth century. The system of mass consumption first developed among those upper-middle-class elements spreading both upward and downward in the course of the twentieth century. In this context, Foucault intelligently argued that to equate sexual repression with the "utilization of labor capacity" in a rather careless Marxoid fashion is to "suppose that sexual controls were the more intense and meticulous as they were directed at the poorer classes." But sexology was first directed against, even as it helped define, the first consumers: the upper-middle classes. In particular, this is important to un-

---

22. For changes in the space of gender and family, see Lowe, *History of Bourgeois Perception*, pp. 70–74, 101–5; for the ambiguity of women's position in the political sphere, at least in the United States, see Paula Baker, "The Domestication of Politics: Women and American Society, 1780–1920," *American Historical Review* 89 (June 1984), 620–47. Baker's article provides a useful context in which to read such American students of sex as Scott, Kiernan, Finck, and Hall.

derstand because sexology was not merely, as Foucault seems to argue, a system of control. It conferred a kind of freedom as well as a set of controls to limit that freedom. Consequently, sexology brought with it a kind of privilege in that it implied a universal democratization and enfranchisement. Still, in historical terms, that privilege was restricted to the class of consumers, which in the late nineteenth century still excluded vast segments of the population.[23]

As a science, then, sexology tended to take the experience of the urbanized classes as universal; as a system of control, as well as a system of freedom, it was applied to middle-class and upper-middle-class men and women, parents and children, heterosexuals and homosexuals. Sexology's insistence on the primacy of the genital zone reinforced not so much bourgeois production as bourgeois reproduction—especially after 1850, at a time of declining birth-rate (long underway in France but more recently begun elsewhere) among the consumer classes, the gradual separation of desire from reproduction, and the beginnings of the emancipation of middle-class women from dependence. Thus, Foucault was right to affirm that "it was in the 'bourgeois' or 'aristocratic' family that the sexuality of children and adolescents was first problematized, and feminine sexuality medicalized." Intellectually, sexology proposed a vision of universal citizenship; practically, at first, few could participate in that citizenship.[24]

23. For the localization of the emerging consumer ideology within the "educated strata in larger cities," see Jackson Lears, No Place of Grace: Anti-Modernism and the Transformation of American Culture, 1880–1920 (New York: Pantheon, 1980), p. 35; for the localization of the sexual aspect of this culture within the middle and upper classes, see Foucault, History of Sexuality, p. 120.

24. Foucault, History of Sexuality, p. 120. Among the factors emancipating middle-class women from dependence within the family, participation in the labor force (measured by the number of married women who worked outside the home) may have been one of the least important. According to Carl Degler, in 1900, "less than 4 percent of married white women . . .

The work of Alfred Kinsey revealed just how long the lower strata of the working classes lived without that consumerist vision of sex which Foucault referred to as "the deployment of 'sexuality.'" In the United States, at least, the Kinsey data suggested a distinction between an expanding "upper-level" erotic culture in which sex was conceived of as desire directed toward the other and a contracting "lower-level" culture in which sex was understood as action. Whereas the narcissistic upper-level culture that Kinsey described appears to have distinguished between heterosexual and homosexual desire and organized sexuality in general on a consensual basis, the "phallic" lower-level culture seems to have differentiated between active and passive roles and tolerated prostitution. It is likely that the "deployment of sexuality" in the course of the twentieth century has contracted the range of the lower-level culture even as it has greatly expanded that of the upper level.[25]

Finally, it must be remembered that the transition from a protoindustrial to an industrial culture was accompanied by tremendous demographic growth, especially in the cities. By 1900, London had grown into a megalopolis of six and one-half million, New York City was at three million, Berlin at two and one-half million and Vienna at one and one-half million. Despite France's demographic "decadence," Paris was also experiencing a population explosion, soaring from 1,400,000 to 3,700,000 during the last half of the nineteenth century. As George Mosse has noted, in the course of the nineteenth century the great city was increasingly feared as a place of evil. In 1907, Charles Hughes, editor of the important American medical journal *The Alienist and Neurologist*, explicitly linked the appearance of perversion and

worked outside the home." See Carl Degler, *At Odds: Women and the Family in America from the Revolution to the Present* (Oxford: Oxford University Press, 1980), p. 384.

25. Alfred Kinsey, Wardell Pomeroy, Clyde Martin, *Sexual Behavior in the Human Male* (Philadelphia: Saunders, 1948), pp. 327–94; and see Paul Robinson, *Modernization of Sex*, pp. 92–99.

lust-murder to the size of cities. Yet, in a sense, I would argue that the sexologists constructed their model of the consuming individual in part from their observation of fundamentally urban people. Indeed, in a way, sexology took the bohemian and pervert as models, grasping the most dramatic manifestations of a rapidly expanding urban life as the rule of all life.[26]

II

In the previous section I tried to explain how political, social, demographic, and economic transformations on both sides of the Atlantic, occurring around the end of the nineteenth century and the beginning of the twentieth provoked the shift in conceptualization among intellectuals evidenced by the emergence of sexology and other contemporary disciplines. At the outset, I insisted that these transformations need not have been thorough to provoke such a shift. Clearly, in the period, say, 1830–1980, there was a tendency toward the erosion of socially significant distinctions between the sexes. Still, even today, these distinctions continue to be very much in evidence. In a sense, then, ideological change may be more thorough than social. At any rate, it appears likely that a *tendency* in the social world is sometimes conceptualized by intellectuals as a *completed shift*.

In the preceding pages, sexology has been presented as a truly transitional ideology, embodying two sets of values. I further suggested that these values may be associated with the transition from a protoindustrial to an industrial culture.

26. For an understanding of sexuality in the city, see Magnus Hirschfeld, *Le troisième sexe: Les homosexuels de Berlin* (Paris: Libraire Medicale et Scientifique [Jules Rousset], 1908); Charles Hughes, "Homo Sexual Complexion Perverts in St. Louis: Notes on a Feature of Sexual Psychopathy," *Alienist and Neurologist* 28 (1907), 487–88; Hull, "Reflections on 'Nationalism and Respectability'"; George Mosse, "Nationalism and Respectability: Normal and Abnormal Sexuality in the Nineteenth Century," *Journal of Contemporary History* 17 (1982), 221; Lears, *No Place of Grace*, pp. 32–46.

Indeed, there is a sense in which these connections appear almost over-determined because two separate aspects of modern industrial culture, mass production and urbanization, both tend to further the development of a consumerist attitude, the first by stimulating idiosyncratic desire and the second by encouraging an anonymous individualism that can border on solipsism.

Nevertheless, I believe that the connections between society and ideology delineated above are probably historical rather than necessary connections. Certainly it would be a mistake to argue for a correspondence between mode of production and social formation as a general law. Specifically, I do not believe that a protoindustrial civilization will always develop an ideology of idiosyncratic production and that an industrial civilization will always elaborate an ideology of idiosyncratic consumption. Indeed, we have every reason to wonder whether individualism need appear at all. Instead, to account for the emphasis on the individual subject implicit in sexology, and earlier, in political economy, and still earlier, in political theory, we must understand how the peculiar logic of Occidental culture dictated an unusual stress on individualism from the beginning. Moreover, the appearance of the sexual category cannot be understood without a knowledge of the structure of political economy, and the emergence and structure of political economy was, I believe, conditioned by the system of competitive states that evolved out of the still earlier decentralized feudal polity. There is, no doubt, a type of determinism here that makes possible a provisional explanation, but it is a excruciatingly complex determinism. At the least, there is the "horizontal" connection between culture and society, which in turn functions only in the context of the "vertical" determination of the past over the present. Consequently, the links between culture and society explored within this chapter make sense only within the long-term historical context of Western culture hinted at in the Introduction.

CHAPTER SEVEN

The Disintegration
of Holism

The purpose of this book has been to situate the science of sex in its larger cultural context in order to illuminate the significance of that science. In part, my argument has implied that the history of Western thought has evinced a tendency toward the gradual elimination of holism. This process involved a continuous redefinition and simplification of holistic functional divisions, in which the so-called ideology of three feudal orders was succeeded in the eighteenth century by a two-function male-female ideology and in the twentieth by what is in effect an egalitarian ideology of consumers united under the single function of desire.[1]

Actually, this process of redefinition appears to be a succession of increasingly less restricted, symbolic definitions of citizenship.[2] Thus, at first, "citizenship" was restricted to members of the first two estates as opposed to the third, a state of affairs modified by the interrelated emergence of the royal bureaucracies and the towns, whose members constituted what was in effect a kind of supplementary nobility.

1. For a further discussion of the first two ideologies and some hint at the third, see Stoianovich, "Gender and Family."
2. Even this must be qualified, because the extension of the democratic model to bourgeois males involved a disenfranchisement of some aristocratic women.

In the seventeenth century, the high/low estate dichotomy was in turn modified by the Lockean distinction between the masculine realm of labor and the feminine realm of family, which further extended the idea of citizenship. This distinction was perfected in the nineteenth century until it was itself modified by the emergence of the sexually differentiated/undifferentiated model that partially accepted the principle of sexual homogenization and thus the symbolic erosion of the barriers excluding women (and perhaps even children) from citizenship, and then by the heterosexual/homosexual duality, which even further accepted the principle of sexual homogenization while continuing to struggle against it.

In short, the long-term tendency in Western culture apparently points in the direction of a dissolution of the idea of hierarchy. It is indeed in this context that a series of "sciences" have emerged, functioning simultaneously to further and resist this dissolution of hierarchy. Moreover, in each case, the process of dissolution has apparently been stronger than the process of conservation, thus permitting the long-term process of democratization to continue. I would further insist that the term "democratization," like individualism, be used in a basically neutral sense, agreeing with Louis Dumont and others that the dissolution of holism permits the possibility not only of greater personal freedom but also of greater state power. But in each case we have, from a purely technical point of view, more individualism.[3]

Sexology has particular significance in this scheme because it appears to be the latest of the ambivalent "sciences" that have emerged in a dialectic with democratization. Sexual science involves the extension of the democratic model to the furthest conceivable limit even as it struggles against this ultimate and apocalyptic dissolution. Involved here is a real sense that the "end of history" is approaching. Even

3. See Dumont, *Essays in Individualism*, pp. 149–79, for an analysis of one form of totalitarianism.

cultural radicals seem to believe it, almost salivating over the possibility of an ultimate and cataclysmic dissolution. Thus, Gilles Deleuze and Félix Guattari discover in Western individualism a democratization that can end only in the disintegration of atomized individuality itself, culminating in an ego-shattering "schizophrenization." Echoing this view, Guy Hocquenghem has envisioned the approaching "sexualization of the world" which "pushes capitalist decoding [democratization] to the limit and corresponds to the dissolution of the human." Indeed, the whole Foucauldian project seems to herald the final "death of the subject."[4]

Clearly, we are here confronted with a problem and we had better admit it. On the one hand, cultural conservatives have always used the threat of dissolution as a justification for preserving particular social orders. Accordingly, one of the central conserving functions of sexology involved the linking of any further democratization to an objective degeneration. In other words, sexologists linked the dissolution of holism within the family to the absolute disintegration of the individual, making this connection by assuming that family structure was a function of individual health. From the perspective of sexology, then, disintegration of relations between individuals was a symptom of disintegration *within* those individuals. It was in fact from this perspective that the consuming individual appeared to be a "dissolute" or "schizophrenized" nonindividual. The sexologists could begin only by conceptualizing the emerging consumer orientation as inhuman, atavistic, or morbid. Thus a concrete historical phenomenon was translated into an eternal, natural one; to discover the "sexonomy" was to conceptualize a social order unknown to political economy, and consequently one that appeared to bourgeois circles as nonhuman.

On the other hand, the extension of the democratic model, heralded by sexology, and ever more evident in the twentieth century, does appear to involve and even necessitate a

4. See Hocquenghem, *Homosexual Desire*, p. 131.

kind of relativization. All the key consumerist values participate in this relativism. The dissolution of need means that
everyone's tastes are in some sense equal; the dissolution
of developmentalism implies that all cultures are somehow
equivalent; and the universal democratization of individuals
appears to remove any formal way of settling disputes between them. Either anarchy or totalitarianism appears on
the horizon; the future seems bleak indeed.

But is not a *kind* of relativism, or at least pluralism, essential to democracy if we take it seriously? Certainly, the dissolution of hierarchy in a formal sense is the whole point. One
thing is certain, though; to sustain any extension of the democratic model, new limits have to be fixed on that model.
Above all, the twentieth century needs a new political philosophy to consolidate the changes that *have* been made. One
way we can move toward such a philosophy is by resisting
the internalization of the bourgeois and transitional models. It is inappropriate to internalize the values of sexology
by seriously speaking of democratization as the "death of
the subject." We have seen, in fact, that the sexologists
themselves began to distinguish in a rudimentary kind of
way between democratization and dissolution by distinguishing between types of degeneration. Psychoanalysis has
to some extent achieved the same separation by distinguishing between the perversion of the whole individual
and the uncoordinated autoeroticism of the dissolved non-
individuality of dementia praecox. Moreover, with Freud's
final elaboration of Eros and Thanatos as supreme instincts,
psychoanalysis advanced as even more profound the distinction between democratization and degeneration, if only
on a symbolic level. In his dichotomization of life and death
instincts, Freud pointed the way to a new psychology and
thus a new system of values which would distinguish between normality and pathology not on the basis of the procreative versus the perverse, the differentiated versus the
undifferentiated, or heterosexual versus homosexual consumption, but on the basis of consumption—Eros—versus

the extinction of consumption—Thanatos. To oppose Thanatos, Freud brought perverse, inverse, and even homosexual consumption over to Eros. This final division drew a qualitative and not merely a quantitative distinction between the (ultimately) life-affirming polymorphous sexuality of the consumer and the deathlike and morbid impulses of annihilation.[5]

But is this the basis for a new morality founded on a revised hierarchy of values? One thing is certain. In constructing his final schedule and distinguishing between Eros and Thanatos, Freud employed a qualitative distinction for the first time. Such a distinction flew in the face of the evolutionary monism in which psychoanalysis and all other systems of "sexual" science were rooted. We have noted that qualitative distinctions are holistic. Precisely for this reason, evolutionary monism's elimination of qualitative in favor of quantitative distinctions between the sexes and thus its elimination of sex differences in favor of sexual differentiation were symbolic of the dissolution of holism in the family and the consequent extension of the democratic model to the furthest limits. Apparently, Freud was in the business of setting a *new* limit by drawing a qualitative, holistic line around all the evolutionary instincts of "sexuality," symbolically banishing to outer darkness the aggressive instincts that menace us all. This dichotomization of life (desire) and death (aggression) represents a defense against further loss of meaning. In a consumerist world, the distinction between life and death may serve as the foundation for a new set of limits permitting a more extensive democratization, without degeneration.

5. Sigmund Freud, *Beyond the Pleasure Principle* (New York: Norton, 1961); Marcuse, *Eros and Civilization*, pp. 222–37.

"The Sexual Counterrevolution" in Historical Perspective

One of the most salient features of intellectual life in the United States today is the convergence of criticism, from left and right, from feminists and antifeminists, directed against that homogenization of the sexes which seems to be inevitable under consumer culture. The so-called sexual revolution has apparently provoked an intellectual (if not actual) sexual counterrevolution, not only among extremists and Sunbelt fundamentalists, but among the most rarified strata of the critical elite. In a revival or pretended revival of older values, a broad spectrum of educated opinion has seemingly turned its back on the future and looked to the past as a source of inspiration.[1]

For the "sexual counterrevolutionaries," whatever their ideological backgrounds, the central feature of contemporary life is its tendency to erode gender. Yet the barely concealed hysteria permeating the literature of cultural conservatism suggests that conservatives do not really believe that gender is here to stay. On the contrary, their work actually appears to be a desperate ideological defense against the imminent

1. Defined broadly, the values of the "sexual revolution" of the 1960s can be understood as an extension and popularization of the consumerist complex of values discussed in the previous chapters. My point is that the sexual revolution was anticipated at the turn of the century in the work of the sexologists and especially that of Freud.

destruction of gender. But by emphasizing that this destruction would be unnatural and false, cultural conservatives can explain how gender may apparently disappear without giving up its fundamental reality. It might happen, they say, in a society that is becoming increasingly unreal.

The very pervasiveness of the sexual counterrevolution necessitates the construction of a new typology (and thus a new theory) of cultural conservatism. The analysis of late-nineteenth- and early-twentieth-century sexology undertaken in the preceding chapters can provide a context for understanding cultural conservatism today. If that analysis is correct, then we should downplay the distinction between the right and the left. Instead, we might perhaps make a distinction between, on the one hand, those conservatives, such as George Gilder on the right and Christopher Lasch on the left, who criticize consumerist values from a productivist or quasi-productivist perspective, and, on the other hand, those conservatives, such as Ivan Illich and Germaine Greer, who reject even this perspective as *too* modern. Whereas Gilder and Lasch partially accept Western culture in emphasizing productivist values, Illich and Greer are much more thorough in their rejection of that culture or at least its postmedieval forms. For these ultraconservatives, consumerist civilization is merely the final phase in the development of the West as an unnatural or demonic anticulture. They argue that the unnaturalness of consumerism is grounded in the equally radical unnaturalness of productivism. For the ultras, indeed, the ideologies of production and those of consumerism are merely two sides of the same unnatural Western coin. Invoking a tradition of sociological manicheanism going back to Burke, the ultras oppose this unnatural culture of the West to the natural civilizations of the third world. In contrast to such a raging critique, Lasch and Gilder appear mere partial or half-hearted conservatives.[2]

2. See also Lawrence Birken, "Review of Ivan Illich's *Gender*," *Telos* 63 (Spring 1985), 219–23.

I

Gilder and Lasch's "partial" critique effectively reproduces the perspective of the productivist ideologies of the seventeenth and eighteenth centuries, in which production for the sake of production was understood as the fundamental value. As we have seen, the emergence of this ideology or family of ideologies in the West signaled the appearance of a conception of individualist production. Production appeared to be emancipated from society in the person of "economic man." In contrast, consumption continued to be understood by many social thinkers as a social or holist phenomenon. That is, needs were understood as "species needs." Classical ideologies (including Marxism) thus opposed individualistic production to social-istic consumption.[3] But in the latter part of the nineteenth and the early part of the twentieth century, a conception of individualistic desire began to become more important, possibly stimulated by a rapidly industrializing and urbanizing civilization. Now from the perspective of the classical ideologies reproduced in the arguments of both rightist and leftist "partial conservatives," this idiosyncratic consumption must appear to be the dissolution of normal socially determined need itself. For Gilder and Lasch alike, consumerist culture is unnatural because it fails to satisfy real "species needs" and because it fails to produce individuals who are aware of these "real needs." Cultural conservatives on the left and the right agree in arguing that consumerist civilization produces only the illusion of liberation through idiosyncratic consumption. In this context, what the right calls "unnatural desires" is what the left calls "false consciousness."[4]

3. See Dumont, *Homo Hierarchicus*.
4. See George Gilder's *Sexual Suicide* (New York: Quadrangle, 1973), p. 241. In some leftist writings, the moral inferiority of consumer culture is often traced to its "artificial" construction. An example of this rather simplistic perspective is evident in Stuart Ewen, *Captains of Consciousness: Advertising and the Social Roots of the Consumer Culture* (New York: McGraw-Hill, 1976). For a more sophisticated critique of the consumerist vision as it appears in economic ideology, see Levine, *Economic Studies*, pp. 175–97.

We have seen that the emergence of a consumerist set of values was specifically marked by the advent of a conception of radically idiosyncratic "sexuality." In this conception, desire was emancipated from its subordination to its socially determined use in reproduction, becoming an end in itself. Precisely because of its transitional nature, sexology since its inception has simultaneously exemplified and struggled against this very desire. Consequently, the work of the sexologists has always been highly ambivalent. Now, Gilder and Lasch alike in effect bemoan the emancipation of idiosyncratic sexuality from the teleology of reproduction. If the former portrays polymorphous perversity as the unnatural desire cultivated by a coterie of intellectuals and radicals, the latter reduces the new sexuality to a manifestation of the false consciousness produced by a coterie of advertising executives and capitalists. Thus the conservative left imitates the right's longstanding preference for conspiracy theories as a defense against the recognition that consumerist civilization and the accompanying dissolution of gender and species need may represent a dialectical development beyond the productivist phase of Western culture. By asserting the conspiratorial (and hence artificial) origins of the new consumerist values, the conservative left attempts to demonstrate that consumerist culture is merely a decadent form of capitalism rather than something new. In effect, the left implies that Western cultures have developed retrogressively beyond the optimum phase for revolutionary and thus moral action. Conversely, only by "regressing" back to productivist values can these cultures reestablish the conditions for true revolutionary consciousness. The conservative left (like the conservative right) accordingly upholds the moral superiority of bourgeois over decadent mass capitalism, preferring a relative restriction to a wide distribution of consumer goods.[5]

5. See Christopher Lasch, *The Culture of Narcissism: American Life in an Age of Diminishing Expectations* (New York: Norton, 1978), and Lasch, *The*

In particular, the conservative left mirrors the right by necessarily preferring the restriction of sexuality to the genital sphere (Wilhelm Reich) rather than its wide distribution in a polymorphous form (Herbert Marcuse). It is in this context that both Gilder and Lasch employ sexology to demonstrate the pathology of polymorphous sexuality under "late capitalism." Here Lasch's psychoanalysis mirrors Gilder's sociobiology. Sexology is thus pressed into service once again; the old intellectual furniture is taken down from the conceptual attic and presented as new. But in understanding sexual science from their productivist perspective, both Gilder and Lasch must distort it by accentuating its conservative side. For the partial conservatives, sexology and psychoanalysis become powerful defenses against the expansion of a consumerist complex of values by explaining that system as the negation of all values. In other words, the partial conservatives have reproduced and strengthened the side of sexual science which explains how the democratization of desire leads to the dissolution of personality, its "sexual suicide" (Gilder) or its contraction into a "narcissistic" selfishness (Lasch). From this conservative perspective on sexology, idiosyncratic consumption appears the result of the dissolution of the "species need" of heterogenitality and the consequent emancipation of idiosyncratic perversity. Of course, one aspect of sexology and psychoanalysis, the aspect incorporated into the writings of the present-day partial conservatives, has always aimed to demonstrate that these idiosyncratic perverse desires are fundamentally a distortion of normal heterogenital need and are consequently "unreal." From this

---

Minimal Self (New York: Norton, 1984), in which he defends his critique of consumerism with some skill (esp. pp. 22–59). For an opposing view, see Abram de Swaan, "The Politics of Agoraphobia," *Theory and Society* 10 (1981), and the series of critical articles following it in the same issue. Also see Daniel Bell's *Cultural Contradictions of Capitalism* (New York: Basic, 1976) for a more sophisticated discussion of consumerism as a contradictory ideology.

perspective, perversion (under which we must subsume any rupture of sex from reproduction) is indeed "false consciousness." But partial conservatives ignore the other more subversive aspects of sexology which has actually contributed to the emancipation of individualistic desire.

In general, the partial conservatives want to reestablish a vanishing holism in the realm of the family. This is implicit in the program of much of the religious right. For example, Enrique Rueda, a critic of polymorphous sexuality who takes a religious (and a Catholic) perspective, has argued against the concept of the "healthy homosexual," reasoning that, however healthy an individual might be, his sexual health can be evaluated only from a social (holist) perspective. The final criterion for health, in other words, is not the individual's self-sufficiency and internal happiness but his contribution to society as a whole. Any deficiency in an individual's contribution to society's reproduction (in both a literal and a figurative sense) thus suggests a deficiency in health. In this context, conservative sexology can function as a secular substitute for religion, replacing the transcendent law of God with an immanent law of nature. Writers such as Alexander Lowen and Arthur Janov start from a psychoanalytic perspective only to distort it radically by jettisoning most of its consumerist elements. This means that they reject the idea of idiosyncratic desire implicit in Freud's thought and uphold the idea of an inborn heterogenitality. Actually, this tendency appears in the leftist writings of Reich, who in effect regarded the idea of the polymorphous perverse as a form of false consciousness. Lowen, in his recent work on narcissism, gives the game away by denying the Freudian concept of a primary narcissism, affirming rather that narcissism is simply the denial of "real" feelings under pathological social and familial conditions. What Lowen is denying is the Freudian idea that human beings are fundamentally narcissistic, polymorphously perverse, genderless consumers in favor of a neo-Enlightenment vision of people as heterogenital reproducers. In his book *The Primal Scream*, Janov holds that the "real people" (those with a true consciousness?) function in a heterogenital manner, whereas unreal people (those with a false consciousness) are perverse and thus dysfunctional. Janov thus denies an instinctual basis for perversion, holding that the "neurotic 'wants'; the normal 'needs'." His entire theory is built upon the assumption that there are "real" individuals with "normal" (species) needs. Thus, Janov really denies individuality to his individuals. In *The Primal Scream*, the pervert is a person who has lost his real needs (heterogenitality, gender identity) as the result of a trauma. Such an individual adopts pseudoneeds in the form of idiosyncratic "wants." Janov's view thus repudiates the insights of sexologists as early as Krafft-Ebing, who recognized the reality of the perverse even if they stigmatized it as primitive.[6]

For the ultras, however, the consumerist and the productivist phases of Western culture are equally damned. In their scheme, sexual science appears a symptom of the very disease it claims to cure. In the recent work of both Illich and Greer, the primacy of heterogenitality upheld by sexology itself becomes a form of perversion. For Germaine Greer, Freud's emphasis on genitality does not ward off so much as it fuels a consumerism intimately connected with capitalism and modernity.[7] In his analysis of sexual science, Ivan Illich similarly concludes that the category "heterosex-

6. In the literature of the mainstream right, consumerist culture (acceptable in its ostensible economic form as a constituent part of capitalism) is criticized when it expresses itself as perverse sexuality. For the religious right see especially Enrique Rueda's *Homosexual Network: Private Lives and Public Policy* (Old Greenwich, Conn.: Devin Adair, 1982), pp. 48–49; for the "pop" therapy of sexual conformity, see Alexander Lowen, *Narcissism: Denial of the True Self* (New York: Macmillan, 1983), whose title gives his argument away, and Arthur Janov, *The Primal Scream: Primal Therapy—The Cure for Neurosis* (New York: Dell, 1972). These ideologies are in themselves not necessarily holistic, but quasi-totalitarian attempts to restore a vanishing holism. The grandiose claims of the "pop" therapists, each of whom claims to have discovered the real nature of humankind, are in effect attempts at "total" solutions that demand the total commitment of the patient to the ideology of the therapist.

7. See Germaine Greer, *Sex and Destiny* (New York: Harper & Row, 1984), p. 234.

ual" is as much a genderless modernity as is the category "homosexual." In other words, the ultraconservatives perceive that even capitalist *normality* is inherently abnormal. But this apparently radical critique of sexology is actually constructed for the highly conservative purpose of thoroughly repudiating the recent and not-so-recent epochs of the West. Perhaps accidently, the profound character of the ultras' critique enables them to grasp more thoroughly the subversive side of sexology. Unlike the partial, the ultraconservatives sense the ambiguity of sexual science and thus its unsuitability as a dependable critique of contemporary sexuality. But this ultraconservativism has some startling implications. Where the partial conservative critique developed by Gilder and Lasch employs sexology to distinguish between normal heterogenitality and abnormal perversity, the ultra critique rejects sexual science itself as a kind of perversity. Because they believe that the very idea of sexuality is perverse, perverse sexuality appears to be less offensive to the ultras. Indeed, Illich and Greer can be comparatively tolerant about the very perversions that seem to terrify Gilder and Lasch.[8]

II

The dissolution of gender that accompanies the transition from a productivist to a consumerist complex of values takes the form of the tendency to treat men and women as interchangeable "individuals." In his recent book *The Minimal Self*, Lasch explains how consumerism drew women and children into previously masculine society as consumers.[9]

8. Illich, *Gender*, pp. 147, 157; Birken, "Review of *Gender*." Also see Illich, *Shadow Work* (Boston: Marion Boyers, 1981). Greer condemns the West for making perversion (the separation of sexuality from reproduction) the dominant mode of "sex," only to advocate the perverse as a means to build a feminist technology of birth-control. For Greer's attitude toward perversion, see pp. 146–47, 234–35; for her attack on sexology, see pp. 236–37.
9. Lasch, *Minimal Self*, p. 186.

But all conservatives seek to establish the impossible and illusory character of this new equality. Sexual counterrevolutionaries thus call for the reestablishment (or preservation) of separate spheres of action for each sex. If women are included in the competitive sphere of action heretofore inhabited by men only, the conservatives warn us, both sexes must be the losers. As both Gilder and Lasch remind us, "feminism" implies an assertion by women of an active desire (consumer choice) that men cannot cope with. Confronted by the consuming woman, they argue, men will either reassert their masculine power by turning violent or give up the last remnants of their masculinity by becoming impotent.[10] Accordingly, feminism is actually dangerous to women, who can best achieve freedom in the Hegelian manner, by submitting.

The ultras' critique of sexual homogenization is merely the intensification of the proposition that the preservation of a system of sexual distinctions best serves justice for women as well as men. But whereas Gilder and Lasch use sexology to show that sexual homogenization is pathological, Greer and Gilder see sexology itself as an example of the pathology (false consciousness) that erodes sexual distinctions. Again, in a sense they are correct; emerging during the transition from a productivist to a consumerist culture, sexology expressed the tendency toward the dissolution of gender even as it struggled against that tendency. But recognizing (if not fully understanding) this ambiguity in sexual science, the ultras employ a more profound mode of criticizing sexual homogenization. For Illich, women become second-rate only when they compete with men. He means to argue that because preindustrial men and women did not compete, they remained in incommeasurable "genders." The sexual inequality of women, he believes, is a function of the attempt to make women equal by including them in the same system of competition as men under industrial society. Illich thus holds that the second-rate status of the feminine

10. Lasch, *Narcissism*, p. 190; Gilder, *Sexual Suicide*, p. 97.

is rooted in the contemporary tendency to compare the feminine with the masculine. In this context, sexism actually appears a function of sexual homogenization. Moreover, any attempt to analyze or compare the sexes within the sane frame of reference (as sexology does) constitutes an ideology of sexual homogenization and is thus sexist.[11] Illich's ideas are strikingly paralleled in Germaine Greer's recent work. For example, his assertion that sexual homogenization degrades women may be compared to her contention that sexual homogenization devalues women by imposing a single, masculine standard of beauty (that of being slim) on men and women alike.[12] It is Illich's parallel argument that the homogenized culture of the industrial world imposes a single, masculine, phallic standard on both sexes, thus rendering the female a second-rate phallusless male.[13] Illich and Greer thus take their stand against the very sociobiologies of sex and population that the partial conservatives employ as defenses against sexual homogenization. For the ultras, these sociobiologies are forms of rather than defenses against that sexual homogenization that judges both sexes by the same standard.

It is within this context that the ultras fall right into line with the current trend toward feminist "separatism." Portraying sexual homogenization (integration) as a universal "masculinization" that reduces women to second-rate men, some feminists have sentimentalized the Victorian culture of the separate spheres. This is sometimes explicit, though more often implicit, in the writings of those feminists who have increasingly opposed the absorption of women into the system of contractual relations, individuality, and citizenship. For these feminists, the feminine realm of the family and home bequeathed to us by our Victorian ancestors appears a separate but equal sphere organized along coopera-

11. For a more thorough discussion of my views on Illich's ideas, see my "Review of *Gender*."
12. Greer, *Sex and Destiny*, pp. 8, 17.
13. Illich, *Gender*, pp. 12–14.

tive rather than competitive lines. But feminist separatism, whatever its radical goals or strategic necessity, may be easily coopted by conservatives who are resisting the tendency toward sexual homogenization. The fetishization of the Victorian sexual categories and the nostalgia for an eroding separate sphere of feminine action cannot be in the long run anything other than the basis for a profoundly conservative critique of contemporary culture. It is easy for the dreams of gendered Victoriana and forgotten Herlands to become the basis for Illich's devastating attack on feminist aspirations to equality. Feminist separatist assertions that the sexual revolution is simply a masculine plot to seduce women easily become the foundation for a thoroughgoing critique of the emancipation of women from the family.[14]

This type of feminist separatism may be subtly reflected in the interesting work of Carol Gilligan, who has attempted to create an alternative and one might say "feminine" form of psychoanalysis. Gilligan argues that there are two possible ways of looking at relationships, one based on the principle of inequality-equality, the other based on the principle of interdependence. She further argues that men tend to view the world in terms of the first principle, women in terms of the second. Her main complaint is that psychoanalysis and psychology in general have taken the male perspective in their analysis of relationships. To redress this imbalance, Gilligan proposes to examine the female perspective.[15]

14. For a discussion of this feminist separatism, see Paul Robinson's "Post-Feminist Fantasies," *Harper's*, March 1983, pp. 71–73. This type of feminism may be pursuing a strategic rationale in recognizing the positive contribution of the feminine sphere and thus rescuing from obscurity the insights gained by women when they were encased in their own domain in the nineteenth-century middle-class family. See, for example, Carol Smith-Rosenberg, "The Female World of Love and Ritual: Relations between Women in Nineteenth Century America," *Signs* 1 (1975).

15. See Carol Gilligan, "Remapping the Moral Domain: New Images of Self in Relationship," paper presented at the Conference on Reconstructing Individualism, Stanford Humanities Center, February 18–20, 1984, pp. 1, 9, 17, 20; and Gilligan, "The Conquistador and the Dark Continent: Reflections on the Psychology of Love," *Daedalus* 113 (Summer 1984).

Gilligan's attempt to construct a new form of psychology may also possess a certain conservative character. Her attempt to tie the inequality-equality perspective to the idea of contractual relationship, and the idea of contractual relationship to masculinity, enables her work to serve as a rationale for a feminist repudiation of the tendency to extend the democratic model to include women. In its place, Gilligan implies that society might be governed by a different principle, one based on interdependence. Moreover, although she starts out by asserting that her principle is merely one of two possible points of view, she ends up suggesting its moral superiority by linking it to love. In a sense, Gilligan is implying that women love better than men and are thus their moral superiors. Women, she seems to be telling us, would be better off not adopting the masculine model. To feminists who repudiate as a masculine plot the extension of individuality to embrace women as well as men, Gilligan's work may suggest an alternative way to organize society. It is an alternative that strikingly resembles Ivan Illich's preindustrial civilization where women and men are supposedly neither equal nor unequal and is perhaps just as mythical. What I suspect that Gilligan may have done is to transform a longing (common to both men and women) for a vanishing sphere of female *dependency* into a concept of *interdependency*. Whatever the case, her work should be of interest to conservatives everywhere.[16]

III

Because the transition from a productivist to a consumerist complex of values has also been associated with the erosion of the distinction between adults and children, cultural conservatives have raised profound questions about the relationship between childhood, child abuse, and

16. Gilligan, "Remapping the Moral Domain," passim.

the sexual revolution in values. The general consensus of cultural conservatives is that the trend toward sexual homogenization apparently characteristic of consumerist culture has involved a sexualization of childhood that is profoundly unnatural and even pathological. For example, Lasch has suggested that a narcissistic culture is dangerous to children, arguing that the emancipation of children by consumerism ultimately left them open "to new forms of manipulation, sexual seduction, and outright sexual exploitation."[17]

Just as some conservatives have questioned whether women might not be better off if they remained outside the competitive sphere, other conservatives have sincerely questioned whether children might not be genuinely better off if they were excluded from this sphere. With some justification, Lasch raises the question whether the democratic model can be overextended. Can we, should we, democratize relations between parents and children? Though Lasch (and his fellow cultural conservatives) argue that this overextension of democracy is responsible for seduction and abuse, it is also possible to argue that the extension of the democratic model to embrace both women and children in fact may have served to make us more aware of their mistreatment. I am simply suggesting, once again, that the sexualization of women and children may have constituted a symbolic representation of their idiosyncratic desire and claim to citizenship. If cultural conservatives see the sexualization of women and children as contributing to their objectification, can we not also see this sexualization as a form of *subjectification*?

The problem of sexualization actually reveals the limitations of the "partial" conservative analysis pursued by Gilder and Lasch. Grounding their critique of consumerism in a sexological perspective, they forget that it was holders of this perspective who first expressed the sexualization of

17. Lasch, *Minimal Self*, pp. 185–87.

women and children. Even by accentuating the conservative side of sexology, they cannot completely eliminate its subversive character. The conservative theoretical context, as well as the immediate perception that child abuse is more common today than in the past, is enough to explain recent interest in the revival of older (and more conservative) models of sexology such as Freud's seduction theory. The current fixation on this theory implies in several ways a conservative repudiation of the long-term intellectual and social trends we have examined in the preceding chapters. By rejecting Freud's oedipal (or counterseduction) theory, writers including Jeffrey Masson and Alice Miller would, whether knowingly or unknowingly, reject the sexualization of the child implied in the Oedipus complex. Moreover, the revival of the seduction theory implies a repudiation of the polymorphous, idiosyncratic desire that fuels the Oedipus complex in favor of the older model of a constant, universal, heterogenital "species need." In place of the relatively new idea that perversion arises from the idiosyncratic desire of the consumer, the reassertion of the seduction theory implies the revival of the older idea that perversion is the result of a seduction that distorts (traumatizes) normal heterogenitality. In this scheme, the origins of perversion are readily found in earlier perversion. Consequently, perversion loses its reality and is revealed to be a form of "false consciousness" once again.[18]

But the ultras' critique is still more thorough. From their perspective, all theories of perversion are themselves perverse. They thus reject all theoretical sexology as a diseased manifestation of "modernity," repudiating not only the more recent consumerist but also the earlier productivist complex of values. Greer and Illich in effect argue that

18. Masson, *Assault on Truth*; Alice Miller, *Thou Shalt Not Be Aware: Society's Betrayal of the Child*, trans. Hildegarde and Hunter Hannum (New York: New American Library, 1984). Whereas Miller has been somewhat ignored in the United States, Masson has been savagely attacked. See Janet Malcolm, *In the Freud Archives* (New York: Knopf, 1984).

Western culture was bad for children long before the emergence of a consumerist mentalité. This distinction between partial and ultraconservative attitudes toward the history of children and childhood is most sharply drawn in analyses of the family. For partial conservatives, the consumerist tendency toward the emancipation (individuation) of women and children as active agents exists in opposition to the existence of the family as a cooperative or holistic institution. The individualism of women and children stands in stark opposition to the holism of the family inherited from earlier epochs. Partial conservatives have addressed this dilemma by upholding the dichotomy between the competitive (masculine) socioeconomic and the cooperative (feminine) familial domain, thus reproducing the bourgeois conception of the separate spheres as a defense against the extension of the democratic, competitive model of society to embrace women and children as well as men.[19]

Accordingly, the partial conservatives take the idea of the bourgeois family, the family that the Oedipus complex simultaneously embodies and subverts, as an eternally true standard with which to measure relations between men, women, and children. Conversely, they take the dissolution or absence of this family in the cultures of the ghetto as evidence of the abortive character of these cultures. In sharp contrast, it is the idea of the bourgeois family that the ultraconservatives condemn as truncated and unnatural. For Illich, this type of family is already an unnatural, "genderless" economic alliance between two types of producers, a man and a woman who is nothing more than a second-rate man. Illich thus sentimentalizes the truly archaic preindustrial "gendered" families he believes once existed in the West and still exist in the Third World. Once again, Greer's

19. In effect, the argument that children and women must be excluded from competition with adult men for their own good appears to reproduce the doctrine of precocity, described above, in an almost unrecognizable form. See Terman, "Precocity and Prematuration."

analysis recalls Illich's. In her recent work, she has criticized the "modern" nuclear family from the perspective of the extended family. Indeed, Greer argues, Western civilization may have never (at least after the Middle Ages) had an extended family. In the bourgeois or Western family, she believes, women are cut off from one another and encased in the "suburban dyad." But in the extended family, women function together because collective and cooperative effort among females from different branches of the family is a necessity. If feminists sentimentalize Victoriana, they should doubly sentimentalize (if Greer is correct) the great patriarchal extended families of the Third World in which women cooperate with other women.[20]

Above all, however, Greer portrays these large extended families (let us assume they exist) as prolife and prochild, in sharp contrast to the antichild, zero-population culture of the sterile West. From both Greer's and Illich's perspective, then, the modern family is not enough of a family to protect the woman and the child from the effects of integration into the competitive sphere of "masculine" life.

IV

A historical analysis such as the one undertaken in the foregoing chapters should shed light on some of these assertions. On the one hand, cultural conservatives are almost certainly right when they argue that the democratic model of society is not universal; on the other hand, they are probably wrong when they imply that this model is masculine in any transhistorical sense. Gilligan, for example, admits that "the representation of the self as separate and bounded [the individualistic perspective] has a long history in the Western tradition."[21] In the preceding chapters, I have speculated

20. Greer, *Sex and Destiny*, pp. 4, 286.
21. Gilligan, "Remapping the Moral Domain," p. 1.

that the origins of this individualistic conception might be traced back to the decentralized political context out of which the civilization of the West emerged. The contractual perspective became explicitly identified with masculinity only in the social thought of Northwest Europe in the seventeenth and eighteenth centuries. Yet the conservatives' whole argument depends upon the postulation of a necessary and thus transhistorical connection between the contractual sphere and masculinity. Because such a connection does not seem to exist, it is impossible seriously to accept the argument that the extension of this sphere to embrace women and children is an unnatural masculinization.

If the gendered ideology associated with early capitalism is, however, taken as eternally true, any tendency toward the dissolution of that hierarchy may be seen as a threat. Conservatives thus uphold the holism of the familiar order as the only alternative to totalitarianism. The argument boils down to the assertion that the emancipation of women and children from "father" (the bourgeois family) only ensures their dependency on the "collective father" (the total state). For many conservatives, universally distributed individualism makes totalitarianism inevitable. But what these conservatives say about the universal individualism of consumerist society others long ago wrote about the more limited individualism of productivist society. For example, Montesquieu argued against the establishment of what we would now recognize as a democracy of property-owning heads of families with as much vehemence as Lasch and Gilder argue against the potential emergence of a more extensive democracy of genderless consumers. Montesquieu reasoned that the liberation of bourgeois individuals would leave them dependent upon the state. Recently, Louis Dumont has explored the close relationship between totalitarianism and freedom, finding them alternative forms of individualistic culture. But if liberalism and dictatorship are simply alternative forms of individualism, then the extension of the democratic model to embrace women and children must imply *both* the possibility of greater freedom and the risk of greater slavery. As a rule, radicals accentuate the first, conservatives the second possibility. In reality, however, each epoch has its good and bad features. In recent decades, a wider diffusion of the consumerist ideology in the form of the so-called sexual revolution has brought the joy of self-acceptance to many, even as it has brought the tragedy of AIDS to others. Sexual freedom is the freedom to be frustrated as well as satisfied, to be a taker as well as a giver, to be diminished as well as enlarged. In the family, self-fulfillment for both husband and wife must be balanced against the drawbacks of divorce. In society, easy access to sexual partners must be balanced against the transience of sexual connections. There are no guarantees. Every revolution is a revolution in values, and there are no revolutions without some bloodshed. Only fanatic ideologues and misguided utopians will characterize the process of democratization as either totally evil or totally good.

Selected Bibliography

Adler, Alfred. *Co-operation between the Sexes: Writings on Women and Men, Love and Marriage and Sexuality*. Ed. and trans. Heinz Ansbacher and Rowena Ansbacher. New York: Norton, 1978.

Altman, Dennis. *The Homosexualization of America*. Boston: Beacon, 1982.

Balbus, Isaac. *Marxism and Domination: A Neo-Hegelian, Feminist, Psychoanalytic Theory of Sexual, Political, and Technological Liberation*. Princeton: Princeton University Press, 1982.

Barraclough, Geoffrey. *An Introduction to Contemporary History*. New York: Penguin, 1967.

_____. *Turning Points in World History*. New York: Thames & Hudson, 1977.

Baudrillard, Jean. *The Mirror of Production*. Trans. Mark Poster. St. Louis: Telos, 1975.

Beard, George. *Sexual Neurasthenia*. New York: Arno, 1972.

Bell, Daniel. *The Cultural Contradictions of Capitalism*. New York: Basic, 1976.

Binet, Alfred. "Le fétichisme dans l'amour." *Revue Philosophique (de la France et de l'Etranger)* 24 (1887).

Birken, Lawrence. "Review of Ivan Illich's *Gender*." *Telos* 63 (1985).

_____. "Darwin and Gender." *Social Concept* 4 (December 1987).

Blaug, Mark. *Economic Theory in Retrospect*. Cambridge: Cambridge University Press, 1974.

Bloch, Iwan. *Anthropological Studies in the Strange Sexual Practices of All Races and All Ages, Ancient and Modern, Oriental and Occidental, Primitive and Civilized*. Trans. Keene Wallis. New York: Anthropological Press, 1933.

———. *The Sexual Life of Our Time.* Trans. M. Eden Paul. London: Rebman, 1909.

Böhm-Bawerk, Eugen von. "The Origin of Interest." *Quarterly Journal of Economics* 9 (July 1895).

———. "The Positive Theory of Capital and Its Critics." *Quarterly Journal of Economics* 9 (January 1895).

———. "The Positive Theory of Capital and Its Critics II," *Quarterly Journal of Economics* 9 (April 1895).

Bukharin, Nikolai. *Economic Theory of the Leisure Class.* New York: International Publishers, 1927.

Bullough, Vern. "Homosexuality and the Medical Model." *Journal of Homosexuality* 1 (January 1974).

Burton, Sir Richard. *The Book of a Thousand Nights and a Night.* 10 Volumes. Vol. 10 ("Terminal Essay"). Benares, 1885.

Carpenter, Edward. *Intermediate Types among Primitive Folk: A Study in Social Evolution.* New York: Arno, 1975.

Chase, Stuart. *The Economy of Abundance.* Port Washington, N.Y.: Kennikat, 1971.

Chauncey, George. "From Sexual Inversion to Homosexuality: Medicine and the Changing Conceptualization of Female Deviance." *Salmagundi* 58–59 (Fall-Winter, 1982–83).

Chevalier, Julien. *Une maladie de la personalité: L'inversion sexuelle: Psycho-physiologie, sociologie, tératologie, aliénation mentale, psychologie morbide, anthropologie, médicine judiciaire.* Lyons: Storck, 1893.

Clark, J. B. "The Genesis of Capital." *Yale Review* 3 (November 1893).

———. "The Origins of Interest." *Quarterly Journal of Economics* 9 (1895).

Clark, Lorenne, and Lynda Lange, eds. *The Sexism of Social and Political Theory.* Toronto: University of Toronto Press, 1979.

Cobbett, William. *Advice to a Young Man.* Oxford: Oxford University Press, 1984.

Cory, D. W. *Homosexuality: A Cross-Cultural Approach.* New York: Julian Press, 1956.

Darwin, Charles. *The Origin of Species by Means of Natural Selection.* New York: Penguin, 1981.

———. *On the Origin of Species: A Facsimile of the First Edition.* Cambridge: Harvard University Press, 1964.

———. *The Descent of Man, and Selection in Relation to Sex.* Princeton: Princeton University Press, 1981.

Davenport, H. J. "Proposed Modifications in Austrian Theory and Terminology." *Quarterly Journal of Economics* 16 (May 1902).

Deleuze, Gilles, and Félix Guattari. *Anti-Oedipus: Capitalism and Schizophrenia.* New York: Viking, 1977.

D'Emilio, John. "Capitalism and Gay Identity." In Ann Snitow, Christine Stansell, and Sharon Thompson, eds. *The Powers of Desire*. New York: Monthly Review Press, 1980.

Dumont, Louis. *Essays on Individualism: Modern Ideology in Anthropological Perspective*. Chicago: University of Chicago Press, 1986.

_____. *From Mandeville to Marx: The Genesis and Triumph of Economic Ideology*. Chicago: University of Chicago Press, 1977.

_____. *Homo Hierarchicus: The Caste System and Its Implications*. Chicago: University of Chicago Press, 1974.

Ellis, H. Havelock. "The Analysis of the Sexual Impulse." *Alienist and Neurologist* 21 (1900).

_____. "Auto-Erotism: A Psychological Study." *Alienist and Neurologist* 19 (1898).

_____. *The Criminal*. London: Walter Scott, 1897.

_____. *Man and Woman: A Study of Human Secondary Sex Characteristics*. New York: Arno, 1974; rpt. ed. of London: Walter Scott, 1904.

_____. "Sexo-Aesthetic Inversion." *Alienist and Neurologist* 34 (1913).

_____. "Sexual Inversion in Women." *Alienist and Neurologist* 16 (1895).

_____. *Studies in the Psychology of Sex*. Vol. 3: *Analysis of the Sexual Impulse, Love and Pain, the Sexual Impulse in Women*. Philadelphia: F. A. Davis, 1904.

_____. *Studies in the Psychology of Sex*. Vol. 4: *Sexual Selection in Man*. Philadelphia: F. A. Davis, 1905.

_____. *Studies in the Psychology of Sex*. Vol. 5: *Erotic Symbolism, the Mechanism of Detumescence, the Psychic State in Pregnancy*. Philadelphia: F. A. Davis, 1906.

_____. *Studies in the Psychology of Sex*. New York: Random House, Lifetime Library Edition.

Ellis, H. Havelock, and J. A. Symonds. *Sexual Inversion*. New York: Arno, 1975.

Engels, Frederick. *The Origin of the Family, Private Property, and the State*. London: Lawrence & Wishart, 1973.

Féré, Charles. *The Sexual Instinct: Its Evolution and Dissolution*. Trans. Henry Blanchamp. London: The University Press, 1900.

Finck, Henry. *Primitive Love and Love Stories*. New York: Scribner, 1899.

Firestone, Shulamith. *The Dialectic of Sex*. New York: Bantam, 1970.

Foucault, Michel. *The History of Sexuality: An Introduction*. Trans. Robert Hurley. New York: Vintage, 1980.

_____. *Mental Illness and Psychology*. Trans. Alan Sheridan. New York: Harper & Row, 1976.

Fraser, W. Hamish. *The Coming of the Mass Market, 1850–1914.* London, Archon, 1981.

Freud, Sigmund. "The Aetiology of Hysteria." *The Standard Edition of the Complete Psychological Works of Sigmund Freud.* Ed. James Strachey, et al. London: Hogarth, 1953–74. Vol. 3.

——. *Beyond the Pleasure Principle.* Ed. James Strachey. New York: Norton, 1961.

——. *The Ego and the Id.* Ed. James Strachey. New York: Norton, 1960.

——. "Formulations on the Two Principles of Mental Functioning." *Standard Edition.* Vol. 12.

——. "On Narcissism: An Introduction." *Standard Edition.* Vol. 14.

——. *The Origins of Psychoanalysis: Letters to Wilhelm Fliess, Drafts and Notes: 1887–1902.* Ed. Marie Bonaparte, Anna Freud, and Ernst Kris; trans. Eric Mosbacher and James Strachey. New York: Basic Books, 1954.

——. *Sexuality and the Psychology of Love.* Ed. Philip Rieff. New York: Collier, 1963.

——. *Sigmund Freud to Wilhelm Fliess 1887–1904, The Complete Letters.* Trans. and ed. Jeffrey Moussaieff Masson. Cambridge: Harvard University Press, 1985.

——. *Three Essays on the Theory of Sexuality.* Trans. and rev. James Strachey. New York: Basic, 1975.

Galbraith, John Kenneth. *The Affluent Society.* Boston: Houghton Mifflin, 1958.

Gilder, George. *Sexual Suicide.* New York: Quadrangle, 1973.

Gould, Stephen. *Ever Since Darwin: Reflections on Natural History.* New York: Norton, 1977.

——. *The Mismeasure of Man.* New York: Norton, 1981.

Greer, Germaine. *Sex and Destiny.* New York: Harper & Row, 1984.

Hays, Carlton. *A Generation of Materialism, 1871–1900.* New York: Harper & Row, 1963.

Hegel, G. W. F. *Philosophy of History.* Trans. J. Sibree. New York: Dover, 1956.

Helmholz, Hermann von. *Selected Writings.* Ed. Russell Kahl. Middletown, Conn.: Wesleyan University Press, 1971.

Hirschfeld, Magnus. *Le troisieme sexe: Les homosexuels de Berlin.* Paris: Jules Rousset, 1908.

Hocquenghem, Guy. *Homosexual Desire.* Trans. Daniella Dangoor. London: Allison & Busby, 1978.

Hughes, Charles. "Homo Sexual Complexion Perverts in St. Louis: Notes on a Feature of Sexual Psychopathy." *Alienist and Neurologist* 28 (1907).

Hull, Isabel. "The Bourgeoisie and Its Discontents: Reflections on 'Nationalism and Respectability.'" *Journal of Contemporary History* 17 (1982).

Illich, Ivan. *Gender*. New York: Pantheon, 1982.

Jackson, J. Hughlings. *Neurological Fragments*. London: Oxford University Press 1925.

Jevons, W. Stanley. *The Theory of Political Economy*. London: Macmillan, 1871.

Kaulla, Rudolph. *Theory of the Just Price: A Historical and Critical Study of the Problem of Economic Value*. New York: Norton, 1940.

Kiernan, James. "Psychological Aspects of the Sexual Appetite." *Alienist and Neurologist* 12 (1891).

———. "Race and Insanity." *Journal of Nervous and Mental Diseases* 12 (1885).

Kinsey, Alfred, et al. *Sexual Behavior in the Human Female*. Philadelphia: W. B. Saunders, 1953.

———. *Sexual Behavior in the Human Male*. Philadelphia: W. B. Saunders, 1948.

Krafft-Ebing, Richard von. *Psychopathia Sexualis—With Especial Reference to the Antipathic Sexual Instinct: A Medico-Forensic Study*. Trans. Franklin Klaf from the 12th German ed. New York: Stein & Day, 1978.

Krouse, Richard. "Mill and Marx on Marriage, Divorce, and the Family." *Social Concept* 1 (September 1983).

Landes, David. *The Unbound Prometheus: Technological Change and Industrial Development in Western Europe from 1750 to the Present*. Cambridge: Cambridge University Press, 1977.

Laplanche, J. and J. B. Pontalis. *The Language of Psychoanalysis*. Trans. Donald Nicholson-Smith. London: Hogarth, 1973.

Lasch, Christopher. *The Culture of Narcissism: American Life in an Age of Diminishing Expectations*. New York: Norton, 1978.

Leach, William. "Transformations in a Culture of Consumption: Women and Department Stores, 1890–1925." *Journal of American History* 71 (September 1984).

Levine, David. *Economic Studies: Contributions to the Critique of Economic Theory*. London: Routledge & Kegan Paul, 1977.

Levine, Lynn. "Dynamics of the Feminine Personality." *Social Concept* 1 (September 1983).

Lombroso, Cesare. *Crime: Its Causes and Remedies*. Montclair, N.J.: Patterson Smith, 1968; rpt. of 1911 edition.

Lombroso, Cesare, and William Ferrero. *The Female Offender*. New York: Philosophical Library, 1958.

Lowe, Donald. *The History of Bourgeois Perception*. Chicago: University of Chicago Press, 1982.

Lydston, Frank. "Sexual Perversion, Satyriasis and Nymphomania." *Medical and Surgical Reporter* 61 (1889).

Macpherson, C. B. *The Political Theory of Possessive Individualism: From Hobbes to Locke.* Oxford: Oxford University Press, 1983.

Mantegazza, Paolo. *The Sexual Relations of Mankind.* New York: Eugenics Publishing, 1935.

Marcuse, Herbert. *Eros and Civilization.* Boston: Beacon, 1966.

Marshall, Alfred. *Principles of Economics.* London: Macmillan, 1907.

Masson, Jeffrey Moussaieff, *Assault on Truth: Freud's Suppression of the Seduction Theory.* New York: Farrar, Straus & Giroux, 1984.

Mayne, Xavier. *The Intersexes: A History of Similisexualism as a Problem of Social Life.* New York: Arno, 1975; rpt. of 1908 private printing.

Menger, Carl. *Principles of Economics.* Trans. James Dingwall and Bert Hoselitz. New York: New York University Press, 1976.

Moll, Albert. *Libido Sexualis: Studies in the Psychosexual Laws of Love Verified by Clinical Case Histories.* Trans. David Berger. New York: American Ethnological Press, 1933.

——. *Perversions of the Sex Instinct: A Study of Sexual Inversion Based on Clinical Data and Official Documents.* New York: AMS Press, 1976; rpt. of Newark: Julian Press, 1931.

Mosse, George. "Nationalism and Respectability: Normal and Abnormal Sexuality in the Nineteenth Century." *Journal of Contemporary History* 17 (1982).

Nicholson, Linda. *Gender and History.* New York: Columbia University Press, 1986.

Ortega y Gasset, José. *The Revolt of the Masses.* New York: Norton, 1957.

Padgug, Robert. "Conceptualizing Sexual Matters." *Radical History Review* 20 (1979).

Raffalovich, Marc. "Uranism: Congenital Sexual Inversion: Observations and Recommendations." *Journal of Comparative Neurology* 5 (1895).

Robinson, Paul. *The Modernization of Sex: Havelock Ellis, Alfred Kinsey, William Masters and Virginia Johnson.* New York: Harper & Row, 1976.

Schrenck-Notzing, Albert von. *Therapeutic Suggestion in Psychopathia Sexualis.* Trans. Charles Chaddock. Philadelphia: F. A. Davis, 1895.

Scott, Colin. "Sex and Art." *American Journal of Psychology* 7 (1896).

Shapiro, Nina. "The Neo-Classical Concept of Capital." *Australian Economic Papers* 20 (June 1981).

——. "The Revolutionary Character of Post-Keynesian Economics." *Journal of Economic Issues* 11 (September 1977).

Stoianovich, Traian. *French Historical Method: The Annales Paradigm.* Ithaca: Cornell University Press, 1976.

——. "Gender and Family: Myths, Models and Ideologies." *History Teacher* 15 (November 1981).

Sulloway, Frank. *Freud: Biologist of the Mind—Beyond the Psychoanalytic Legend.* New York: Basic, 1983.

Susman, Warren. *Culture as History: The Transformation of American Society in the Twentieth Century.* New York: Pantheon, 1984.

Terman, Louis. "A Study in Precocity and Prematuration." *American Journal of Psychology* 16 (1905).

Williams, Rosalind. *Dream Worlds: Mass Consumption in Late Nineteenth-Century France.* Berkeley: University of California Press, 1984.

Zaretsky, Eli. *Capitalism, the Family, and Personal Life.* New York: Harper & Row, 1976.

——. "Male Supremacy and the Unconscious." *Socialist Revolution* 21–22 (January 1975).

Index

Library of Congress Cataloging-in-Publication Data

Birken, Lawrence, 1951-
  Consuming desire.

   Bibliography: p.
   Includes index.
   1. Sex customs—United States—History—19th century. 2. Sex
customs—United States—History—20th century. 3. Sexual eth-
ics—United States—History—19th century. 4. Sexual ethics—
United States—History—20th century. 5. Sex. I. Title.
HQ18.U5B57 1988   306.7 '0973   88-47719
ISBN 0-8014-2058-X